Henry Barclay Swete

Church Services

and service-books before the Reformation

Henry Barclay Swete

Church Services
and service-books before the Reformation

ISBN/EAN: 9783337295103

Printed in Europe, USA, Canada, Australia, Japan

Cover: Foto ©Lupo / pixelio.de

More available books at **www.hansebooks.com**

CHURCH SERVICES

AND

SERVICE-BOOKS

BEFORE THE REFORMATION.

HENRY BARCLAY SWETE,
D.D., LITT.D.,
REGIUS PROFESSOR OF DIVINITY, CAMBRIDGE.

PUBLISHED UNDER THE DIRECTION OF THE TRACT COMMITTEE.

LONDON:
SOCIETY FOR PROMOTING CHRISTIAN KNOWLEDGE,
NORTHUMBERLAND AVENUE, W.C.; 43, QUEEN VICTORIA STREET, E.C.
BRIGHTON: 129, NORTH STREET.
NEW YORK: E. & J. B. YOUNG & CO
1896.

THE following pages are based upon a course of lectures delivered to candidates for Ordination. They are published in the hope that the subject may be of interest not only to young students of Theology, but to the many lay members of the Church of England who thank GOD for the Book of Common Prayer.

The best thanks of the writer are due to the Librarian of Cambridge University, for permission to reproduce pages from two of the MSS. under his care; and to the Rev. Chr. Wordsworth, Prebendary of Lincoln and Rector of Tyneham, who has read the proofs, and suggested some valuable additions to the notes.

H. B. S.

CAMBRIDGE, *Whitsuntide*, 1896.

CONTENTS.

CHAPTER I.
THE BOOK OF COMMON PRAYER AND THE OLD
SERVICE-BOOKS 7

CHAPTER II.
THE BREVIARY 26

CHAPTER III.
THE MISSAL. 74

CHAPTER IV.
THE MANUAL 122

CHAPTER V.
THE PROCESSIONAL 172

CHAPTER VI.
THE PONTIFICAL 192

NOTES 211

INDEX 225

ILLUSTRATIONS.

		PAGE
1.	Reproduction of two pages of an Antiphonary in the possession of the author	52
2.	Reproduction of a page of the York Manual (Camb. Univ. Lib. Ee., iv. 19)	152
3.	Reproduction of a page from the Winchester Pontifical (Camb. Univ. Lib. Ee., ii. 3)	204

CHAPTER I.

THE BOOK OF COMMON PRAYER AND THE OLD SERVICE-BOOKS.

WHITSUNDAY, June 9, 1549, witnessed the beginning of a new era in the public worship of the English Church. On that day throughout the land the " Book of the Common Prayer and Administration of the Sacraments and other Rites and Ceremonies of the Church after the Use of the Church of England" superseded all Service-books previously allowed. From that day "all and singular Ministers in any Cathedral or Parish Church or other Place within this Realm of England, Wales, ... or other the King's Dominions," were "bounden to say and use the Mattins, Evensong, Celebration of the Lord's Supper, commonly called the Mass, and Administration of each of the Sacraments, and all their common and open Prayer, in such Order and Form as is mentioned in the same Book and none other or otherwise [1]." Before the end of the year a royal proclamation required the surrender of the Service-books hitherto authorized, and all that were surrendered were defaced or destroyed, with the view of securing the complete abolition of the ancient services [2].

The Act of Parliament which legalized the new book was entitled "An Act for the Uniformity of Service and Administration of the Sacraments throughout the Realm." Uniformity in public worship was its professed end, and the uniformity at which it aimed was the establishment of a truly national rite. During her previous existence of nearly a thousand years the Church of England had failed to provide a national Use. She might have possessed one from the first had Augustine of Canterbury followed the advice which, if Bede may be trusted, he received from Gregory in answer to a question which he had himself addressed to the Pope upon this very point. The members of the Roman mission had heard the Gallican mass during their sojourn in Gaul; and the services chanted at St. Martin's, Canterbury, in the presence of

[1] 2 & 3 Edw. VI. c. 1 (Jan. 22, 1549).
[2] Maskell, *Mon. Rit.* i. p. clxxii f.

Queen Bertha by her Gallican chaplain, Bishop Liudhard, were doubtless of the same type; whilst early associations led the missionaries to prefer the offices which they had used at Rome. Augustine, eager for uniformity, inquired why it was that, the Faith being one, the customs of Churches differed so widely. Gregory took a larger view of the whole question. He was so far from desiring the triumph of a single Use, that he proposed to add to the existing varieties one especially adapted to the wants of the new Church. Uniformity was desirable in a national Church, but not uniformity based upon rigid adherence to the customs of either Gaul or Rome. "It is my pleasure[1]," he replied, "that anything you find which is likely to be especially acceptable to Almighty God, whether in the Roman, Gallican, or any other Church, be pressed into the service of the Church of England while she is still young in the Faith. Things are not to be esteemed for their connexion with places, but places for the sake of things. Whatever things in the several Churches are godly, helpful to devotion, or right in themselves, let these be collected and delivered to the

---

[1] Bede, *H. E.* i. 27 (Notes, p. 211).

English people, to be treasured by them as their use." M. Duchesne doubts the genuineness of this document, and is disposed to attribute it to Archbishop Theodore († 690), or one of the scholars who surrounded his person[1]. If we accept this view, the words are of even greater interest, for they will then point to a desire for a national liturgy on the part of the leaders of the Church of England a full century after the conversion of Kent. But the wise and liberal scheme, whether it proceeded from Gregory or from Theodore, was not destined to be realized at the time. It remained inoperative, until it bore fruit in the work of Archbishop Cranmer, whose first Book of Common Prayer might almost seem to have been moulded upon this project of the sixth or seventh century.

The Church-books of Celtic Britain appear to have perished in the troubles of the Saxon invasion; not a vestige of any of them is known to exist[2]. But if we may judge of them from the few books of Scotch or Irish origin and somewhat later date which have survived, their offices were akin to those

---

[1] Duchesne, *Origines du Culte Chrétien*, p. 94.
[2] See Warren, *Celtic Liturgy*, esp. p. 163 ff.

which were used in Gaul¹. More than once after the withdrawal of the British Church, the Celtic or Gallican type of worship reappeared in England. At Canterbury, as we have seen, Augustine found a Gallican bishop in possession of St. Martin's. The Celtic missionaries who re-evangelized Northumbria, followed their native Use, and at Lindisfarne, under Aidan, Finan, and Colman, the mass was doubtless nearer to the Gallican than to the Roman form, while at Dunwich the Gallican rite was probably practised by Felix, the apostle of East Anglia, who came from Burgundy². In Kent, on the other hand, Augustine and his successors seem to have followed Roman ways. The Roman psalmody (*cursus psallendi*) and the Roman canon of the mass naturally came in the train of the Roman mission, notwithstanding Gregory's wiser counsels, if indeed they may be traced to Gregory. In the North, too, after the departure of Colman, Roman influences were predominant, and the Celtic services gradually disappeared³. Great efforts were made to instruct the Northumbrian clergy in Roman

---

[1] See Warren, pp. 68, 75.
[2] Bright, *Early Engl. Ch. H.* pp. 130, 151.
[3] Bede, iv. 5, 18. Cf. Batiffol, *Histoire du Bréviaire Romain*, p. 79; Warren, p. 76.

Church music and to secure the use of at least the canon of the Roman Mass; and in the main these efforts were successful [1]. Still, the Celtic and Gallican customs died hard. The Anglo-Saxon Mass, with the exception of the canon, did not altogether follow Roman lines. Besides special commemorations, *missae*, and rubrics, it possessed a wealth of proper prefaces unknown to the Gregorian mass, and episcopal benedictions for which there was perhaps no Gregorian precedent. Such pre-Norman Service-books as the Leofric Missal, and the Missal of Robert of Jumièges, archbishop of Canterbury (1051–1052), bear witness to the presence of non-Roman elements in the English liturgy before the Conquest. But if the services of the Church of England were not purely Roman, they did not attain to the character of a national Use. In each diocese there were local customs which grew into separate Uses. "Heretofore," so Cranmer writes in 1549, "there hath been great diversity in saying and singing in Churches within this realm; some following *Salisbury* Use, some *Hereford* Use, some the Use of *Bangor*, some of *York*, and some

---

[1] Comp. the 13th and 15th Canons of the Council of Clovesho (Haddan and Stubbs, iii. p. 367).

of *Lincoln*." The original diversity was accentuated and fixed through the strengthening of the secular cathedral bodies which followed the Conquest. Within a few months, during the year 1090-1, the three great churches of York, Lincoln, and Salisbury received new constitutions from the Norman prelates placed over them by William [1]. These strong centres of ecclesiastical influence were able to impress their own customs upon the other churches of the diocese and in some cases to exercise this influence far beyond diocesan limits. Other cathedral bodies followed the example, and beside the Uses mentioned in Cranmer's preface, St. Asaph, Ripon, Lichfield, Exeter, Wells, Winchester, and St. Paul's, London, are known to have had distinct customs in Divine service [2]. From the thirteenth century, however, the Use of Sarum began to predominate. It was introduced during that century at Wells and Exeter. St. Paul's adopted it in 1415, and Lichfield a little later on: in 1542 the Convocation of Canterbury imposed the Sarum Breviary on the whole of the southern province. Thus, for three

---

[1] C. Wordsworth, *Lincoln Cathedral Statutes*, p. 33 f. Cf. Prothero, *Memoirs of H. Bradshaw*, p. 280 f.
[2] Maskell, *Liturgy, &c.*, p. lxii.

centuries before the Reformation the Church of England had been feeling her way towards the Uniformity which was at last attained in the Book of Common Prayer.

The Sarum Use, as the immediate predecessor of our present offices, deserves special attention. It is commonly ascribed to Osmund, Bishop of Sarum (1078–1099); but the attribution must be received with some reserve. Osmund was a nephew of the Conqueror, and a man of affairs: he filled the office of Chancellor of England, and had served as one of the Commissioners who compiled Domesday Book [1]. As bishop he rendered two conspicuous services, founding a cathedral at Old Sarum, and giving a constitution to its chapter. His relation to the Use is less certain. It is said that his attention was called to the matter by a riot at Glastonbury in 1083, which followed an attempt on the part of the Norman abbat to thrust upon his monks a new mode of Psalmody. Such an event may well have determined a far-seeing prelate such as Osmund to place the customs of his new cathedral on a definite basis; but it certainly would not have dictated the policy of adopting an entirely

---

[1] W. H. Jones, *Fasti Eccl. Sarisb.*, p. 39 f.

new Use. The Use of Sarum was doubtless largely pre-Norman, and Osmund's work limited to the infusion of a Norman element, and the codification of the whole. The *Consuetudinarium* or Custom-book, formerly attributed to Osmund, has been traced by Mr. Bradshaw to a later prelate, Richard le Poore, who was Bishop of Salisbury from 1215 to 1242. Bishop Poore founded a new cathedral at Salisbury (1218), and appears to have further emulated his great predecessor by giving a permanent form to the traditions which had grown up round the name of the founder of the old church at Sarum. At any rate the popularity of the Sarum Use seems to date from the episcopate of Poore, and his name deserves to be associated with that of Osmund in connexion with the Diocesan Use which was destined to be the parent of the Use of the whole Church of England.

Next to uniformity of worship the English reformers of the sixteenth century had at heart the unification of the Service-books. The *Consuetudinarium* of a cathedral body was a single book[1], but the services it regu-

---

[1] For the contents of the Sarum Consuetudinarium see *Lincoln Statutes*, p. 67 f.

lated filled a series of MSS., some of which were of considerable bulk, and indeed were usually broken up into several volumes. Before the Reformation the English parish priest needed at least four great Church-books[1]—a Breviary for use in the choir, a Missal for the services of the Altar, a Manual for the occasional offices, and a Processional for the periodical processions which took place in the church or churchyard, or on certain days in the streets of the town and the lanes of the adjacent country. But in practice a much larger number of books was required. The Breviary was a compilation, and to some extent a compendium, of the liturgical Psalter, the Antiphonary, the Hymnal, the *Legenda*, the Collect-book. Even this list does not exhaust the books employed in the divine office; the *Diurnale* or book of the Day Hours, the *Ordinale* or *Fica* or Pie, the *Lectionarium*, *Legendarium*, and *Passionale* were often written in separate MSS. for use in the choir. The Missal, again, included the Epistle-book, the Gospel-book, the *Graduale* or Grail, the Troper, as well s portions of the Sacramentary; and these

---

[1] See the admirable note by Mr. Bradshaw printed in Mr. Prothero's *Memoir*, p. 443 f.

components were often produced separately for the various officiants. Decrees of English Diocesan Synods and constitutions of the Metropolitan continually press upon parishioners the duty of procuring these costly books. Thus Walter Gray, Archbishop of York (1250)[1], directs that the parish churches be provided "in the way of books with *legenda*, antiphonary, grail, psalter, troper, ordinale, missal and manual." A similar list is given in a constitution of Robert Winchelsey, Archbishop of Canterbury (1305). The larger churches required or procured several copies of the chief books; thus an inventory of the Church of All Saints, Derby, in the year 1466, mentions eight Antiphonaries, four Processionals, two Missals, three Grails, two Manuals, two *Ordinalia*. Church accounts of the first half of the sixteenth century enable us to estimate the burden entailed upon the parishes of England by the necessity of providing these numerous Service-books and keeping them in repair. The accounts of Stratton, Cornwall, contain the following entries between 1526 and the death of Mary: "Item paid for ii processionalles ii$s$. iii$d$. ... Item p^d. for

---

[1] Wilkins, *Conc.* i. 768.

18 CHURCH SERVICES AND SERVICE-BOOKS.

a manuele ii*s*. [1526]... Item p^d. for a newe manuele book ii*s*... Item p^d. for a newe processionale book xx*d*. [1535]... Item p^d. for a manuele boock xxii*d*. [1547]... Item p^d. for a processional and a whole manuell vii*s*. [1554][1]." It seems as though a new Manual and a new Processional were required in this small Cornish parish every ten or twelve years; frequent use in the churchyard and parish explains why these books needed more frequent renewal than the others. A new Missal or Great Breviary does not seem to have been needed at Stratton during a period of twenty-eight years. But the cost of these larger volumes must from time to time have fallen heavily on the country parishes, even when the price had been reduced by the art of printing. To parishioners as well as to clergy it was a matter for congratulation to know that for the future two books would generally suffice. The preface to the new Prayer Book calls attention to this point: " by this order the Curates shall nede none other bookes for their public services but this book and the Bible; by the means whereof the people shall not be at so great charges for bookes

[1] Maskell, *Rit. Mon.* i. p. xix.

as in tyme past they have been[1]." Yet Cranmer could not have foreseen the full extent of the benefit he had conferred upon the English people. The Book of Common Prayer has not only saved the pockets of parishioners and lessened the labour of "Curates"; its compactness has made it possible to put a complete copy of the Services of the Church into the hands of her youngest and poorest member. No conceivable revision of the old Service-books in their separate form would have attained this end. The practical genius of the nation calls for a compendium of Divine worship which may satisfy the needs of all Englishmen, and the Book of Common Prayer supplies the demand. The old Service-books were written almost exclusively for the use of the clergy; the layman was content with the "little Office" to be found in the Latin *Horae*, or in the English Primer[2]. The Prayer Book is as much the layman's companion as the priest's, and it has largely taken the place of private

[1] The price of the new Prayer Book was limited by royal authority: "the King's Maiestie... strictly chargeth and commandeth that no maner of person do sell the present booke unbounde above the price of ii shyllinge and ii pence the piece. And the same book in paste or in boordes not above the price of three shillings and viii pence the piece."

[2] Some account of these Service-books for the laity will be found in the Notes (p. 211 f.).

manuals of devotion, whilst in church it is in the hands of the whole congregation. Something has doubtless been sacrificed to brevity, but the result has been to secure for the Church of England the most popular Service-book in Christendom.

Even more important than the unification of the Service-books was the simplication of their contents. The abandonment of the Latin tongue was an important step in this direction. There was much to be said in favour of the use of Latin in the mediaeval books. The Church of England had said her offices in Latin from the beginning. The Celtic Churches had done the same; in Ireland, Scotland, and Gaul, Latin was the Church tongue long before the national Use had been superseded by the Roman Mass and the Roman Hours, and there is no reason to doubt that it was the tongue in which the British Church had worshipped God. Moreover it is not to be denied that the Latin language was singularly well adapted to the devotions which it assisted; there is much in the mediaeval books which would lose its chief beauty if it were rendered into the vulgar tongue, and one can only wonder at the courage which attempted the translation of a portion of their contents, and the skill which succeeded so well. But Cranmer saw that there could be no "common prayer" in the full sense of the words until the services were said in a language which the whole nation understood. So long as he had in view merely a revised Breviary for the use of the clergy, the Archbishop adhered to the traditional Latin; but as soon as the idea of daily congregational worship had been clearly grasped, he abandoned it without hesitation. "The service in this Church of *England*," he complains, "these many years hath been read in Latin to the people, which they understood not . . . here you have an Order for Prayer as touching the reading of the Holy Scripture . . . a great deal more profitable and commodious than that which of late was used." It was not surprising that the Church had found it impossible to secure the attendance of the laity at the daily prayers when they could not understand what the Priest sang or said. Yet there were other causes for their indifference beside the use of a dead language. Even if they could have understood it, the Breviary appealed only to the monk or to the priest; an expert was needed to thread its mazes; the laity were warned off not merely by the Latin dress of the offices, but by their complexity. Even for the clergy "to turn the Book only was so hard and intricate a matter that many times there was more business to find out what should be read, than to read it when it was found out." Exquisite as was the skill which had framed the system of "Anthems, Responds, Invitatories, and such like things," it had no voice to reach the heart of the people; the elaborate care, the scientific precision with which the fabric was raised defeated the end of the builders, and the musical setting, designed to evoke and interpret the thought wrapt up in psalm or lesson, served only to "break the continual course of the reading of the Scripture." The clergy may have suffered in some degree by the sweeping away of the old system, and the artistic beauty of the offices has certainly been diminished. But the cost had been counted, and it seemed to Cranmer and his friends to be light in comparison with the gain. We have lost the finished perfection of the mediaeval services, but we have gained a Book of truly common prayer. The canonical Hours have been abandoned, but in place of them a daily Order of Morning and Evening Prayer, in which priest and people worship God together, has been restored. The canonical Hours had become in England, as they are still in countries where the Church has not undergone reformation, practically a dead letter for all but the monastic bodies and the priesthood: the Order of Morning and Evening Prayer is a living rite for which thousands of the English laity can bless GOD. "In one country alone," it has been truly said, "in one form alone, does the ancient Western Office really survive... The English Church is in this matter the heir of the world. She may have diminished her inheritance, but all other Western Churches have thrown it away [1]."

Of the purification of the old offices little is said in Cranmer's preface. They were less deeply dyed in the peculiar theology of the mediaeval church than is commonly supposed. The substance is largely taken from Scriptures or the Fathers, or consists of devotions framed within the first six centuries. The Preface to the new Prayer Book is singularly fair in this matter; it speaks of the "uncertain stories" which had found their way into the Saints' Day lessons, and of many things left

---

[1] Freeman, *Principles of Divine Service*, i. p. 279. See also Neale, *Essays*, p. 46.

out, "whereof some be untrue, some vain and superstitious." But these accretions fell away naturally and without any organic change, when the services were submitted to the test of Scripture and of history. The offices, as a whole, with few exceptions, were free from objections on this score. So far were the English Reformers from condemning any devotional form on account of its use by the mediaeval Church, that in several instances, as we shall see, they have followed mediaeval practice where it differs from that of earlier times, or retained a formula which was unknown to either West or East before the eleventh or twelfth century. Their quarrel with the Church of the Middle Ages was limited to matters in which its innovations were inconsistent with the primitive truth.

The revision of the Service-books which resulted in the Book of Common Prayer was certainly thorough and fearless. Yet it was a revision only and not a substitution of new offices. Nearly all that was of permanent value, and at the same time capable of adaptation to the altered circumstances of the Church, has been scrupulously retained. No sober son of the Church of England can regret that this is so. The Prayer Book owes its strength and beauty mainly to the Service-books which it has displaced. There are indeed elements in the present Book which are due to the Reformers of the sixteenth century, and there were such in the first Book of 1549. But as a whole the Prayer Book is a remodelling, under the new influences which the Reformation called forth, of the manifold materials which had been placed at the disposal of the Church by fifteen centuries of devotional life. The new Order firmly rooted itself in the past, whilst it opened great possibilities in the future. He who would understand it aright must not only be in general sympathy with the purposes and hopes of the Reformers; he must prepare himself for the study of their work by following the course of Christian worship from the earliest times.

Our aim in the following pages will be to examine the history and contents of each of the great liturgical collections which have contributed their store to the "Use of the Church of England," and to compare their services with those which correspond to them in the Book of Common Prayer.

CHAPTER II.

THE BREVIARY.

The Prayer Book opens with an "Order for Morning and Evening Prayer, daily to be said and used throughout the year." In the Book of 1549 these offices were described as Mattins and Evensong, and these titles survive in the headings to the tables of Proper Lessons for Sundays and holy days. The old names carry with them associations to which the English services do not altogether correspond, but they serve an important purpose if they lead Englishmen to connect the present Order with the daily worship offered by their forefathers, and thus bear witness to the continuity of the Church's devotional life.

It has been truly said that the ideal of the Christian life is perpetual fellowship with God, maintained by acts of prayer as frequent as possible[1]. To the Apostolic age this

---

[1] Duchesne, *Origines*, p. 431.

ideal was new, for it is a product of the Faith of the Incarnation. But the Christian practice of consecrating certain moments in the day to acts of prayer was inherited from ancient Israel. Devout Jews, from the age of the Captivity at least, had been accustomed to pray three times a day[1]. The offering of the morning and evening sacrifice supplied two fitting opportunities for prayer; a third was found either at noonday or at the hour of sunset[2]. The first generation of the Church adopted the custom; Peter and John "went up into the temple at the hour of prayer, being the ninth hour"; at Joppa Peter "went up upon the housetop to pray, about the sixth hour." The tradition outlived the separation of the Church from the synagogue and the destruction of the temple, and was maintained by Gentile believers as well as by those of Jewish origin. The *Didache*[3], after reciting the Lord's Prayer, directs that it be offered thrice a day. Clement of Alexandria bears witness that there were Christians in his day who, while endeavouring to maintain a constant spirit

[1] Ps. lv. 17; Dan. vi. 10, 11.
[2] J. Lightfoot, *Hor. Hebr.* iv. p. 37; Schürer, *Jewish People*, &c., II, i. p. 290, *n.* (E. T.); Blass, on Acts iii. 1, x. 9.
[3] C, 8.

of prayer, set apart certain hours, such as the third, sixth, and ninth[1]. Tertullian recognizes the practice as existing at Carthage, and commends it; the third, sixth, and ninth hours seemed to him to be doubly appropriate, both as dividing the day into four equal portions, and because they are assigned to prayer in Holy Scripture and by the example of the Apostles[2]. In Cyprian's time the "Apostolic hours" were well established in the regard of the African Church, and mystical reasons for their observance had already suggested themselves: the triple devotion pointed to the Trinity in GOD; the particular hours were connected with the chief events of Christian history—at the sixth hour Christ hung upon the cross, at the ninth He died, at the third the Spirit descended[3].

The Apostolic Hours find no place in our Book of Common Prayer, nor does it appear that they were marked by any public services in the age of Cyprian. Their observance was left to the discretion of individuals, who added these hours at pleasure to their other seasons of private devotion. Not the day-

---

[1] *Strom.* vii. 7. 14.   [2] *De Orat. Dom.* 24; *de Jejun.* 10.
[3] *De Orat. Dom.* 34 sq. Miniatures of these events occur in some of the Breviaries.

light, but the night seems to have been chosen for the earliest non-eucharistic worship of the Church. The night services known as "Vigils" were doubtless suggested by the frequent calls to watchfulness uttered by our Lord and His Apostles. Christ had represented the interval between the Advents as a single night, during which His servants must keep incessant vigil [1]. The vigil service was a response to His command, expressed in the form of a definite act. But it was not at any time a daily service; its observance was connected with the approach of an holy day. Easter Day had its vigil almost from the first, and Tertullian refers to the difficulty which a Christian woman married to a pagan would find in reconciling her husband to her absence from home during the night before the Paschal solemnity [2]. The solemnity of the Easter vigil was deepened by a tradition that the Second Coming of the Lord would surprise the world on some Easter Eve [3]. After a time the weekly Lord's Day claimed the same honour, and every Saturday night was marked by a vigil service; other solemn days were distinguished in the same way, as,

[1] E. g. Mark xiii. 35. [2] *Ad Uxor.* ii. 4.
[3] Lactant. *Div. Instit.* vii. 19. Jerome on Matt. xxv. 8.

for example, the weekly *stationes* or fasts of Wednesday and Friday, and the yearly commemorations of local martyrs, which in some Churches after the middle of the third century must have added largely to the number of these nocturnal gatherings. But vigil services, however multiplied, were nowhere of daily occurrence, and though they may have yielded suggestions for the arrangement of the regular night Hours, it is precarious to assume a direct connexion between two systems which differed in this fundamental point.

The night Hours were more probably the outcome of private acts of devotion [1]. "Besides the hours observed from ancient times" (writes St. Cyprian, shortly after A.D. 250) "both the seasons and the mystical reasons for prayer have grown upon us in these days—in the morning we must pray, to celebrate the Resurrection of the Lord . . . as the sun sets and the day comes to an end prayer must be offered again . . . that the True Light may return to us . . . the shadows of night need bring no intermission to our prayers, for when are we left without light if we have the true Light in our hearts? We

[1] Cf. The *Church Quarterly Review* for Jan. 1896, art. v.

who are ever in Christ, Who is the Light, ought not to desist from prayer even during the night hours [1]." The *Canons of Hippolytus*, which have been taken to represent the practice of the Roman Church early in the third century [2], reveal the beginnings of a Church order in connexion with these frequent devotions. "Let every one be careful to pray earnestly at midnight, for our fathers have taught us that at that hour all creation is ready for the service of the Divine Majesty, and the angelic ranks and the souls of the just bless God; and the Lord testifies that at midnight a cry was heard, 'Behold the Bridegroom cometh, go ye out to meet Him.' Again, at the hour of cockcrowing prayers are to be offered in the churches, since the Lord says, 'Watch ye, for ye know not at what hour the Son of Man cometh, whether at cockcrowing or in the morning.'" Other canons in this collection prescribe prayers on rising from sleep, at the Apostolic Hours, and at sunset. Every Christian is to make it his business to attend

---

[1] *De Orat. Dom.* 35.
[2] So Achelis (in Gebhardt and Harnack's *Texte u. Untersuch.* 6, vi). On the other hand Funk, *Die Apostol. Konst.*, assigns these canons to a later date. The question is briefly discussed by Mr. A. C. Headlam in the *Guardian* of Feb. 12, 1896 (p. 243).

public prayers whenever they are held in the church, or if he cannot do this, to read and pray at home at the accustomed times [1]. Similar rules seem to have been observed in Egypt and the East during the third and fourth centuries. Thus the second book of the *Apostolical Constitutions* directs the Bishop to exhort his flock to come to church daily at daybreak and in the evening, adding, however, that this was specially to be desired on Saturdays and Sundays [2]. The eighth book provides an order of common prayer for these two hours; four others, the Apostolic Hours and the hour of cockcrowing, are to be observed by the bishop in private, if he finds it impossible to assemble the faithful at church [3]. At Jerusalem, near the end of the fourth century, Silvia found four public services a day in the Church of the Holy Sepulchre, mattins (*gallicinium*), sext, none, vespers (*lucernarium*), to which terce was added in Lent [4]. But the Church of the Anastasis at Jerusalem possessed unique associations, and it was Holy Week when Silvia was present at its services; moreover the congregation

---

[1] Achelis, *Die Canones Hippolyti*, p. 131 f.
[2] C. 59.   [3] C. 33.
[4] Gamurrini, *S. Silviae Peregr.* p. 45 f.

consisted partly of monks and virgins, partly of pilgrims such as Silvia herself; the attendance of the laity at the night hours was voluntary and limited ("viri aut mulieres, qui tamen volunt maturius vigilare"). At Constantinople the laity, as Chrysostom complains, satisfied their consciences by assembling in church once a week, and even then found it hard to leave their worldly cares behind them [1]. St. Basil indeed opened the churches of his diocese for the night services, and defended his action by appealing to the practice of the Churches in Egypt, Palestine, Syria, and the further East [2]. But it may be doubted whether many were attracted beyond the members of the coenobite communities. To men of the world the hour was prohibitory, even if a desire for daily common prayer were felt beyond the monasteries. It was the tendency of the age to concentrate Christian life in religious houses; the leaven was being rapidly withdrawn from the lump, and the mass of the baptized retained little more than the form of godliness.

With the habit of assembling in church for daily common prayer a fixed order of service came into use. "At the hour of cockcrowing,"

[1] *Serm. de Anna*, iv. 1.   [2] *Epp.* ii. 207 (Notes, p. 212).

the Hippolytean canons prescribe, "let the presbyters, subdeacons, and readers assemble in the church daily, together with the whole people, and betake themselves to devotion, to psalmody, the reading of the Scriptures, and prayers[1]." Perhaps the earliest extant forms are those provided in the eighth book of the *Constitutions* for the morning and evening services[2]. Each office begins with a fixed Psalm; bidding prayers for the various ranks in the congregation, from the Catechumens to the faithful, are recited by the Deacon; then the Bishop offers prayer and gives his blessing. The precise form may be ideal, but the general order doubtless corresponds with the practice of the Syrian Churches in the fourth century. St. Basil's description of a night service, though it enters less into details, is more interesting, as the account of an eye-witness:

"Among us the people go at night to the house of prayer, and in distress, affliction, and continual tears make confession to God. At last they rise from their prayers and begin to sing psalms. And now, divided into two companies, they chant antiphonally . . . afterwards they again commit the prelude of the strain to one of their number, and the rest

---
[1] Achelis, p. 122. [2] Cc. 33-41.

take it up; and so, after passing the night in various psalmody, praying at intervals, as the day begins to dawn all together as with one voice and one heart raise the Psalm of Confession (Ps. li.) to the Lord [1]."

Not less attractive is Silvia's picture of the services at Jerusalem: "From cockcrowing to daybreak hymns are said and psalms and antiphons sung responsively, each hymn being followed by a prayer. When the day has begun to dawn, the Mattins hymns are sung. Then the Bishop comes with the clergy... and offers a prayer for all... this done, he blesses the catechumens, and after another prayer, the faithful [2]." Similar services followed at sext and none. At Vespers the church is lit up, and the Psalms of the Hour of Lighting (*psalmi lucernarii*) are said, together with their antiphons. Then comes a bidding prayer with *Kyrie eleison*, chanted at intervals by a large choir of boys. The Deacon conducts this litany; and when it is over, the Bishop prays and gives the benediction as at the end of the early service.

But it was in the monasteries that the Hours found their natural home; only those

---

[1] *Epp.* ii. 207 (Notes, p. 212).
[2] Gamurrini, p. 45 f. (Notes, p. 212 f.)

whose lives had been consecrated to this special type of religious life were able to maintain the constant round of prayer. Consecrated virgins and monks formed, as we have seen, the bulk of the congregation at the daily services which were held in the churches; and where the churches failed to provide opportunities, they held similar services among themselves. Thus the writer of the tract *On Virginity* attributed to Athanasius, directs the virgin, whether alone or in company with others, to rise at night and repeat the fifty-first Psalm and as many other Psalms as can be said standing, each Psalm being followed by confession and prayer, with an Alleluia after every third. At dawn Psalm lxiii. is to be recited, and after it *Benedicite* and the *Gloria in Excelsis*[1]. Among the Egyptian monks, according to Cassian, it had been the immemorial custom to recite twelve Psalms at Vespers and twelve at Nocturns; after the Psalms came two lessons, one taken from the Old Testament, the other from the New, except on Saturdays and Sundays, when both came from the New[2]. Elsewhere the number of the Psalms sung at Nocturns varied according to the custom

---

[1] Migne, *P. G.* xxviii. c. 276.   [2] *Instit.* ii. 4 sq.

of the brotherhood; some monastic bodies sang twenty or thirty Psalms each night, while others were content with eighteen; others, again, regulated the psalmody by the length of the night[1]. Thus the monks of the Irish Bangor, in the seventh century, between Nov. 1 and March 25, sang half the Psalter on Saturday night and the other half on Sunday: between March 25 and June 24 the number was diminished weekly by three Psalms; whilst after midsummer it was increased weekly in the same proportion till it attained the maximum again. On the other nights of the week the number varied from thirty-six Psalms to twenty-four[2].

In the Egyptian monasteries, down to the fifth century, the brethren met but twice in the twenty-four hours for common prayer; the other hours were observed by private devotions in their cells. On the other hand, the religious of Syria and the East assembled for the Apostolic Hours, reciting three Psalms at each[3].

As monasticism spread westwards, Eastern practice began to colour the Western observ-

---

[1] *Instit.* ii. 2.
[2] Warren, *Bangor Antiphonary*, ii. p. xi f.
[3] Cassian, *Instit.* iii. 289.

ance of the Hours. But the introduction of the Eastern arrangements into the West was largely due to the zeal and enterprise of an individual. Early in the fifth century John Cassian, a Western, as it appears, and probably a native of Gaul, who had spent the early years of his life in a monastery at Bethlehem, and afterwards studied the monastic systems of Egypt and the desert, came to settle at Marseilles, in the heart of a country where monasteries abounded on every side. Here Cassian wrote his *Institutes of Coenobitic Life*, in which he expounded to the Latin West the principles of Eastern monasticism, dealing in the second and third books with the night and day services (*de canonico* (1) *nocturnarum*, (2) *diurnarum orationum et psalmorum modo*). From this work we are able not only to gather the Eastern and Egyptian order, but to see how far it had begun to prevail in the West. Cassian tells us, for example, that a Mattins service at daybreak instituted in the monastery at Bethlehem was "now very generally observed in the Western countries." This new service of dawn, he observes, made up the number of seven Hours, in conformity with the Psalmist's declaration, "Seven times a day do I praise Thee." The night services consisted of Nocturns, Mattins, and Lauds; at daybreak came the supplementary Mattins, roughly corresponding in point of time with the service elsewhere known as Prime[1]; the Day Hours followed in due course, and Vespers ended the services of the day.

Cassian's work in South Gaul was continued by Caesarius and other Gallican prelates who issued Rules for their monastic institutions. Side by side with the monastic observance of the Hours, we have evidence of the existence in Gaul of secular services following similar lines, and moulded by Eastern influences. At Milan, also, the Eastern type seems to have prevailed. The Roman system, as reflected in the Rule of St. Benedict, who followed its main features, is in many ways distinct. The Hours are the same, except that St. Benedict adds an eighth, *completorium* or Compline, a last office at night before retiring to rest. But the services differ from those of the Gallican monastic rules in some important points. On the nights when Vigils were anciently kept, the Mattins consist of three Nocturns.

---

[1] *Instit.* iii. 4. The usual identification with Prime is disputed by a writer in the *Church Quarterly Review* for Jan. 1896, and is perhaps not technically correct.

Scripture lessons are read at each Nocturn, and *capitula*, or short chapters, assert the principle of Scripture reading at the other Hours. The fixed Psalms of the day Hours are not read in their course at Nocturns and Vespers, so that the daily recitation is incomplete. Above all, the Roman services are distinguished by their rich store of antiphons and other variable devotions [1].

According to Eastern practice the recitation of the Psalms, whether in churches or in monasteries, was musical in character. The historian Socrates tells us that tradition ascribed the invention of antiphonal singing to Ignatius of Antioch [2], and the story may be taken to mean that the practice began in the monastic communities which grew up around the Syrian metropolis. From Antioch it spread westwards. Basil enthusiastically describes the responsive singing of the Cappadocian Nocturns [3]; Chrysostom found it in use at Constantinople; at Milan it flourished under the sympathetic guardianship of St. Ambrose. Augustine, who had heard the Psalms recited in Africa or at Rome to the old plain song, was captivated by the new music, although

---

[1] *Church Quarterly Review* for Jan. 1896, p. 417 f.
[2] *H. E.* vi. 8.   [3] *Epp.* ii. 207.

his judgement pronounced at first in favour of a simpler style[1]. The slight intonation which resembled reading rather than singing, and of which the great Athanasius was believed to have been the author, seemed to him better adapted to the sober gravity of Divine worship. Yet he confessed that the new system had advantages of its own, winning weaker brethren to devotion by the delight which it ministered to the ear.

Rome held out longer against the innovation. The Psalms were still recited there after the manner of reading, or with some slight inflexion. But the change seems to have come early in the fifth century; in the *Liber Pontificalis* it is attributed to Pope Celestine (422–432), who ordered the Psalms to be sung before Mass; a later text adds the word *antiphonatim*, representing Pope Celestine as the first to direct antiphonal recitation of the Psalter[2]. The Rule of St. Benedict refers incidentally to the Roman psalmody, and another entry in the *Liber Pontificalis*[3] credits Pope Hormisdas (514–523) with the instruction of the Roman clergy in the new style of musical

---

[1] *Confess.* x. 33.
[2] Batiffol, *Histoire du Bréviaire Romain*, p. 43 ff.
[3] i. 269.

recitation. Putting together these slight hints, we may infer that efforts were made at Rome from the fifth century to establish in the churches a daily musical service. Another Roman book, the *Liber Diurnus*[1], which, though a compilation of the eighth century, contains older materials, affords a curious illustration of the fact. A "suburbicarian" bishop is represented as promising the Pope, "I will keep daily vigils in the church, with all my clergy, from first cockcrowing to daybreak; during the shorter nights, from Easter to the September equinox, three lessons antiphons and responds shall be recited, and from the September equinox to Easter, four. On Sundays, at every season, we promise to offer to God nine lessons with their antiphons and responds." Psalmody is not mentioned here, but it formed, of course, in the early Roman as in all other nocturns, the backbone of the service; the lessons antiphons and responds being secondary and depending on it. It is interesting to observe that the antiphonal singing of the Psalms has brought with it a system of musical adjuncts, *the antiphonae* or anthems attached to the Psalms, and the

[1] iii. 7.

responsoria or responds which followed the lessons.

The erection of monastic communities in connexion with the parishes (*tituli*) of Rome supplied the parish churches with clergy at liberty to conduct the daily offices, and qualified by their training in music to do so. Under the care of the basilican monks the day Hours were duly sung in the Roman churches; terce, sext, and none, each had its appropriate office, and before the end of the eighth century prime and vespers were added to the list [1]. Meanwhile, a school of ecclesiastical music (*schola cantorum*) was formed, and Rome, though at the outset she had been anticipated by Antioch, Constantinople, and Milan, became the instructress in this art of Western Europe. The Roman school of music was reproduced both in England and among the Franks; it was the ambition alike of the Gallican and Anglo-Saxon Churches to "sing the Psalms as they are sung at Rome" (*sicut psallit Romana ecclesia* [2]).

We have dwelt at some length on the history of the Hour services at Rome, because the Roman offices of the sixth and seventh

---

[1] Batiffol, p. 63 f. [2] *Ib.* pp. 50 f., 79 f.

centuries supplied the groundwork of our own mediaeval Breviaries. Augustine and his colleagues, being Roman monks, brought with them to Kent the Roman Hours, and sang them daily in St. Martin's Church. "In this church," writes Bede, "they first began to assemble for worship, to sing the Psalms (*psallere*), pray, celebrate mass, preach and baptize; thus imitating the apostolical life of the primitive Church, which served the Lord in frequent prayers, watchings, and fastings[1]." Whatever doubts the missionaries may have felt with regard to the introduction of the Roman mass and the Roman baptismal office, they could not have hesitated to retain the Roman "Psalm-course" (*cursus psallendi*), seeing that the keeping of the Hours must have been at first practically limited to the clergy. Their daily services need not have interfered with the Gallican Hours, which were still perhaps maintained at St. Martin's by Bishop Liudhard; but the Gallican Use would naturally disappear in the next generation. In the north of England it was otherwise; Celtic methods of dividing and singing the Psalter doubtless prevailed in Northumbria till the influence of Wilfrid and

[1] *H. E.* i. 26 (Notes, p. 213).

Benedict Biscop turned the scale against them. Before the time of Bede there was already in the Northumbrian Church a passion for everything Roman. Benedict, on one of his visits to Rome, brought back with him no less a person than the precentor (*archicantor*) of St. Peter's, John, abbat of the Vatican monastery of St. Martin, sent by Pope Agatho to England for the express purpose of teaching the *cursus* as it was sung before the Pope. Precentor John took up his quarters at Wearmouth, whither representatives of nearly all the Northumbrian monasteries flocked to learn the Roman rite. The instruction was given orally, but John also left written directions, and copies of these were still to be found in the time of Bede at Wearmouth and elsewhere. From Bede's account we gather that they offered guidance upon all the details of the Hour services, the daily distribution of the Psalter, the lessons, the *ritus canendi*, embracing no doubt all the musical portions of the services, the antiphons and responds as well as the setting of the Psalms, and lastly the *circulus anni*, i.e. the changes required by the incidence of the seasons and the holy days[1]. It was doubtless in the

[1] *H. E.* iv. 18 (Notes. p. 213).

monasteries that the labours of the Roman precentor bore most fruit. But serious attempts were made to introduce the Hours into the churches, and to bring the laity together to the services. Among the *excerpta* ascribed to Egbert, Archbishop of York (732–766), but of later origin, we find the following stringent rules:

> "All priests at the proper Hours of day and night are to ring the bells of their churches, and celebrate the sacred offices."
>
> "Our fathers ordained seven services (*sinaxes* = συνάξεις) to be sung daily . . . the clergy are bound to observe these Hours as they occur day by day."
>
> "If any cleric or monk, being in health of body, shall neglect his vigils and daily offices, let him be deprived of communion."
>
> "If any cleric on hearing the bell do not at once hasten to the church, he shall be subject to censure."

Before his ordination the priest was, according to the same authority, to provide himself with his "tools," including a Psalter, Lectionary, and Antiphonary, the books necessary for performing the daily offices. As for the laity, their attendance was simply invited by the ringing of the church bells, but they were expected to come at least to the Saturday evensong, with which the Sunday services began. So completely was the system naturalized in Anglo-Saxon England, that the

Hours received English names; our forefathers in days before the Conquest spoke of *uht-song* (Mattins), *after-song* (Lauds as distinguished from Mattins), *prime-song, undern-song* (Terce), *midday-song* (Sext), *none-song, evensong* (Vespers), *night-song* (Compline)[1].

We may now proceed to consider the books which were needed for the recitation of the daily services. Three have already been mentioned incidentally. The Psalter was of course indispensable, except for those of the monks and clergy who knew the Psalms by heart. These were perhaps the majority; indeed, canons exist which refuse admission to the priesthood or episcopate of those who could not recite the Psalter from memory. Under these circumstances one or two copies of the Psalter might suffice for a monastery or church. But, as time went on, the ecclesiastical Psalter was by no means limited to the Psalms of David; it had come to include a mass of other liturgical matter more or less nearly connected with the singing of the Psalms. Even the fifth century MS. Bible, known as the Codex Alexandrinus, contains at the end of its Psalter a collection of Scriptural canticles,

---

[1] Cp. Rock, *Church of Our Fathers*, iii. pt. 2, p. 1 f.

followed by the *Gloria in Excelsis* (ὕμνος ἑωθινός), which, as we have seen, formed a part of the night office recommended to consecrated virgins by the writer of the Athanasian tract on Virginity. These canticles were sung at the Mattin-lauds, and it was customary to annex them to Psalters written for liturgical use. Other additions followed; thus the great Canterbury MS. of the eighth century, known as the Psalter of St. Augustine (Vesp. A. 1), contains hymns as well as canticles, whilst a later hand has added the *Te Deum* and the *Quicunque*, with certain prayers. The next step was to include the antiphons and responds connected with the night Hours, and for the convenience of the reader these were not relegated to an appendix, but dovetailed with the Psalms. We shall return to this point when we come to the Psalter of the Breviary; for the present it is sufficient to note the tendency to swell and complicate the Psalter by the insertion of foreign matter.

The Antiphonary, as a book connected with the services of the Hours, contained the antiphons to the Psalms, and the responds and verses which followed the lessons; the hymns, little chapters, and other musical portions of the offices were often added. An antiphon is a sentence appointed to be recited before a Psalm or group of Psalms and repeated at the end. It seems to have had its origin in the prelude which struck the keynote and began the melody of the musical setting[1]. In singing the prelude the precentor used a few words taken from the Psalm itself or based upon it, and the clause thus selected to begin and end the antiphonal rendering acquired from it the name of *antiphona*. But if the antiphon originated in the exigencies of antiphonal singing, it soon acquired another and more important office. As the music of the antiphon prepared the choir for the singing of the Psalm, so its words fixed the sense in which the Psalm was to be understood on each occasion[2]. An example or two will make this clear. In the Sarum Mattins for Christmas Day the first nocturn or portion of the Psalter proceeded thus: "*Antiphon*. The Lord said to me, Thou art My Son, this day have I begotten thee.—Psalm ii. *Antiphon*. As a bridegroom the Lord cometh from His chamber.—Psalm xix. *Antiphon*. Grace is

[1] Gevaert, *La Mélopée Antique*, p. 84.
[2] Cp. Neale, *Essays on Liturgiology*, p. 15 f.

poured upon thy lips, therefore God hath blessed thee for ever.—Psalm xlv." On Easter Day the second Psalm occurs again at Mattins, but its antiphon is changed to an Easter note:

> "I asked my Father. Alleluia.
> He gave me the nations. Alleluia.
> For mine inheritance. Alleluia."

In its earliest phase the antiphon seems to have been intercalated between the verses of the Psalms as well as recited at the beginning and end. This arrangement survived in the anthems appropriated to the *Venite*, known as Invitatories. The Invitatory was repeated nine times during the course of Ps. xcv. Perhaps it was owing to the weariness which this repetition induced that the Prayer Book of 1549 directed the *Venite* to be "said or sung without any Invitatory." The Invitatory, however, relieved the monotony of the daily *Venite*, giving to it a special colouring on each day of the week, and at each season of the year. Thus in the Sarum ferial Mattins the Invitatories are varied in the course of the week as follows:

Monday.—" O come let us sing unto the Lord."
Tuesday.—" Let us heartily rejoice in God our Saviour."

Wednesday.—" In Thy hands, O Lord, are all the corners of the earth."

Thursday.—" Let us worship the Lord, for He hath made us."

Friday.—" The Lord Who hath made us, O come let us worship."

Saturday.—" The Lord our God, O come let us worship."

The seasons brought yet greater variety, connecting the opening words of the Psalm with the fact commemorated. Thus the Advent Invitatory, " The King, Who is to come, the Lord, O come let us worship," was exchanged on Christmas Day for ". Christ is born to us : O come," &c. ; whilst on Easter Day it became " Alleluia, Alleluia, Alleluia : the Lord is risen again. Alleluia, Alleluia."

The responds to the Lessons were selected with equal skill, and served the purpose of assisting meditation upon the short passages of Scripture which preceded them, while at the same time they supplied materials for a musical setting which enhanced the beauty of the service. Sometimes these *responsoria* filled a separate volume known as the *Responsoriale*, but their usual place was in the Antiphonary, where they followed the antiphons in the order of the Sunday and weekday services throughout the year.

It will be readily understoood that the

mediaeval Antiphonary was a book of considerable size; indeed it was usually necessary to break it up for binding into several MSS. Not only were the contents voluminous, but for the convenience of the precentor and the choir both words and music were written in as large and bold a hand as possible. A volume in the writer's possession, containing the antiphons, &c., from the octave of the Epiphany to the first Sunday in Lent, consists of 134 pages measuring 24 × 16 inches, and the letters are four-sixths of an inch in length; and many of the books written for great churches or monasteries were on a yet larger scale. Earlier MSS. of this class in which the musical notes were simply *neumes*, i. e. notes dotted above the words without the use of lines, were less bulky, but the book must always have been costly, and the difficulty of providing copies for the parish churches considerable [1].

The Lectionary contained the lessons to be read at Mattins. Of such a collection some early copies survive; in Sir E. Maunde Thompson's *Manual of Palaeography* [2] the student may see specimens of handwriting from a Luxeuil Lectionary dated A. D. 669 and another

---

[1] See c. i.   [2] p. 228.

ANTIPHONS, ETC.
ANTIPHONARY (IN THE POSSESSION OF THE AUTHOR).   [To face p. 82]

written at Monte Cassino in the eleventh century. The *Lectionarius* was properly a book of Scriptural lections only; the entire corpus of Mattins lessons known as the *Legenda* includes patristic and hagiological extracts. For these, separate books were usually needed: the *Sermologus* and *Homiliarius* supplied the patristic sermons and expositions, the *Legendarius* contained the Acts of the Saints, the *Passionarius* the sufferings of the Martyrs. Sometimes in place of the *Lectionarius* the reader used the Bible, significantly described as the *Bibliotheca*—in itself a library of books[1].

Yet this account does not exhaust the books used in the singing of the daily offices. The office hymns were gathered into the *Hymnarium*, the collects into the *Collectarium*, and it would be easy to add to the list. It is not of course to be inferred that all these books were to be found from the eighth century onwards in every church or monastery, or that the collections were everywhere uniform in their contents or bore identical names. But there was a tendency from the first to gather the several factors of the daily offices into separate codices, in which the

---

[1] Cp. Maskell, *Dissertation on Service Books* (in *Mon. Rit.* i. p. xxii f.); Procter and Wordsworth, *Sar. Brev.* iii. p. xxiv f.

more homogeneous elements were grouped together at the pleasure of the compilers, but more or less after a traditional and conventional way.

One is almost surprised that no effort was made during the great ecclesiastical revival of Charlemagne's time to bring these collections into a single and portable form, a *Breviarium* or compendium of the daily offices, as it was afterwards called. But the idea did not suggest itself, or it was abandoned as impracticable. A *Breviarium* was indeed drawn up by Alcuin for the use of the court, but it was merely a book of private devotions, quite distinct from the monastic and ecclesiastical services of the Hours[1]. Charles made it his business to supply the clergy with amended copies of the lessons, and for this end he intrusted the revision of the Vulgate to Alcuin, and that of the *Homiliarius* to Paul the Deacon. But the very natural step of gathering the whole mass of devotional literature connected with the Hours into one codex, seems not to have been taken before the end of the eleventh century. At least, the earliest known manuscript of this kind is dated in the year 1099[2].

---

[1] Batiffol, p. 194.   [2] Id, p. 195.

It bears the title *Incipit Breviarium sive Ordo officiorum*, and contains the Psalter and canticles, the hymns of the daily offices, the collects, the antiphons and responds, the *capitula* for the day Hours, and the lessons and responds proper to certain classes of saints. It is not a complete collection, for the lessons for Sundays and ordinary week-days are wanting, but, so far as we know, it is the first book of the kind; and it is worthy of notice that this earliest Breviary, like the system of Hours which it aimed at codifying, had its birth in monastic surroundings, for it was written in the Benedictine house at Monte Cassino. Rome found it convenient to accept the principle of the Breviary; from the beginning of the fourteenth century we find MSS. bearing the title *Breviarium secundum Usum Romanae Curiae*.

In England the common Breviary was known by another name. Our Norman forefathers called it the *Portiforium*, the book, that is, which the priest carried with him when he went upon his travels (*liber quem portat secum foras*). In Anglo-French this word became *portehors*; in the vernacular it degenerated into porthos, portos, portuisse, portasse, portous, and other forms. The name was already used in the thirteenth century; a visitation of the Treasury of St. Paul's in the year 1295 mentions among the books of the cathedral church *unum portiforium plenarium*, a complete Breviary or portos. Yet the word *breviarium* was not entirely superseded by *portiforium*; the latter, as its derivation indicates, belonged in strict use to the portable book which was the constant companion of the ecclesiastic; the former was chiefly employed for the great MSS., written for use in choir, which gave the Mattins lessons at full length. But the Great Breviary was a comparatively rare book. While more than fifty editions of the Portifory were issued from the press between 1475 and 1557, only five editions of the Great Breviary are known (Venice, 1494-5; Rome, 1496; London, 1506; Paris, 1516 and 1531)[1]. The smaller book was the one which the laity were accustomed to see in the priest's hand, and the numerous corruptions of *portehors* which occur in English texts show how familiar the word must have been to all classes of the English laity[2].

It was the Breviary or Portifory of the

---

[1] Procter and Wordsworth, *Sarum Breviary*, iii. p. xli f.
[2] Maskell, i. p. lxxxvii f.

THE BREVIARY.   57

Church of Salisbury (*Breviarium secundum Usum Ecclesiae Sarum*) which supplied our Reformers with the basis of their reconstruction of the daily prayers. This book, which had become extremely scarce and dear, has recently been reprinted by the Cambridge University Press, under the editorship of two eminent liturgical scholars, Messrs. F. Procter and C. Wordsworth. It will be convenient to use the Cambridge edition in describing the contents of the Sarum Breviary.

The Breviary contained the Hour services of the year arranged under four heads, the Psalter, the " Proper of Time," the " Common of Saints," and the " Proper of Saints." To these we must add the Kalendar and the " Ordinale " or " Pie," which were necessary as guides to the use of the book [1].

The Sarum Psalter, as we have already hinted, was far from being, like the Psalter of the Book of Common Prayer, a mere transcript of the Book of Psalms, divided into sections, to be said or sung in rotation during a certain period of time. It contained, in fact, the substance of the services for the Sundays and week-days throughout the year,

---

[1] Procter and Wordsworth, *Sarum Breviary*, ii. p. viii f.

so far as the daily services were not affected by special provision for the season or for the holy days. In other words the Breviary Psalter was, in liturgical language, the "common of time" for the Hours; it supplied everything that was essential to the services apart from the special requirements of particular days, all that was common to all days alike. All the Hours found a place in the Psalter, for the recitation of Psalms is the principal feature in every one of the daily offices. But the Psalms were sung in regular course only at Mattins and Vespers, just as since the Reformation they are said and sung in course at Morning and Evening Prayer. Before the Reformation the course was weekly, and instead of the Psalms being resumed at Evensong at the point where the choir had broken off at Mattins, they were divided into two sections (Ps. i–cix, cx–cl), of which the first was reserved for Mattins, and the second for Vespers. The other Hours had fixed Psalms assigned to them, and after the Roman practice these Psalms were passed over at Mattins and Vespers, when they occurred in the daily course. Moreover, the weekly course was constantly interrupted by the preference which was given to the Psalms proper to the season or to a holy day, so that the recitation of the Psalms was by no means so regular as a hasty glance at the Psalter of the Breviary would lead the student to suppose. As a matter of fact, as Dr. Neale points out, "a few of them were repeated over and over again, and the rest left utterly unsaid [1]." Mattins alone had the distinction of possessing lessons, the others Hours, Vespers included, having only *capitula*, i.e. short sentences from the Epistles, rarely exceeding a verse in length [2]. But the Mattins lessons were not in the Psalter, for they belonged to the "proper of time," being variable not merely with the day of the week, but from day to day throughout the year.

We are now prepared to examine the structure of the daily services. Each office begins, after private devotions, with sentences nearly corresponding to those which still stand near the beginning of our Order of Morning and Evening Prayer. After the sentences at Mattins follow the *Venite*, a Hymn, the Psalms in the order

---

[1] *Essays*, p. 13.
[2] In cathedral, collegiate, and monastic houses, certain lections were attached to prime.

of their course, with Lessons after each Nocturn of Psalms, the whole being ended on festivals by the *Te Deum*. At Lauds, Vespers, and Compline, the sentences are succeeded by the Psalms (fixed, at Lauds and Compline, but at Vespers recited in their course), a *capitulum*, hymn, canticle and *preces* or suffrages. At Prime, Terce, Sext, and None the order is: Sentences, Hymn, fixed Psalms, *capitulum, preces*. Thus while all the services have certain common elements, each group is distinguished by features peculiar to itself, as well by the order in which the common elements occur. Mattins stands alone, marked by its *Venite* and Lessons; Vespers, which shares with Mattins the daily course of the Psalms, agrees in structure with Lauds and Compline, all the three possessing a Gospel canticle; Prime, and the Apostolic Hours are without the canticle and differ in arrangement from both the other groups [1].

Passing from structure to matters of detail, we note that Sunday Mattins consisted of three nocturns, the first of which contained twelve Psalms, grouped under three Glorias

[1] See Mr. W. C. Bishop's useful tables in P. and W. (iii. p. xxxii).

and Antiphons, while to the second and third were assigned three Psalms each. On other festivals nine Psalms were sung, each having its own *Gloria* and Antiphon; on ordinary week-days (*feriae*) twelve Psalms, under six Glorias and Antiphons. Each group of Psalms was followed by three Lessons, i.e. by a Lesson divided into three sections, every section being preceded by a benediction and followed by a respond. Thus on Sundays there was ordinarily eighteen Psalms and nine Lessons; on week-days, not being festivals, twelve Psalms and three Lessons; on festivals, not being Sundays, nine Psalms with three lessons or nine, according to the number of Nocturns. Eastertide and Whitsuntide were distinguished by having only one nocturn at Mattins, with three Psalms and three Lessons. When there were three nocturns, the first system of lessons was generally taken from Holy Scripture, and the passages were consecutive or chosen on the ground of some common reference; thus the lessons of the first nocturn on Advent Sunday were Isa. i. 1-4, 5-9, 10-15, and those of the first nocturn of Christmas Day, Isa. ix. 1-8, xl. 1-11, lii. 1-10. For the second and third systems, patristic expositions or homilies were commonly used, and on Saints' Days, the lives of the saints and passions of the martyrs. Each lesson was preceded by a benediction and followed by a respond.

Lauds began after the last lesson, or on Sundays and festivals after the *Te Deum*, which on those days followed the lessons. Nominally, Lauds had five Psalms, each followed by its *Gloria*; but the fourth "Psalm" consisted of the Old Testament canticles, and the fifth of Pss. cxlviii–cl, the *laudes* (αἶνοι) with which in the early days of monasticism it had been customary to greet the break of day. A *capitulum* and a hymn followed the Psalms; then came an invariable Gospel canticle, the *Benedictus*, and the office ended with suffrages and a collect (*oratio*). Prime and the three next Hours had also their fixed Psalms; for Prime were appointed Pss. xxii–xxvi, lv, cxviii, and the last two sections of Ps. cxix, the remainder of the last-named Psalm being divided between Terce, Sext, and Nones. A distinguishing feature of Prime in England was the daily recitation of the Athanasian Creed; it was marked also by its lengthy suffrages.

The vesper Psalms were five in number, recited as at Mattins in regular course.

The invariable canticle of Vespers was *Magnificat*; *Nunc Dimittis* was reserved for Compline. Compline appears in the Sarum Psalter under twenty-two different forms, corresponding to the seasons of the Church year. With Lauds and Vespers it has a Gospel canticle: like Prime it possesses a wealth of *preces*; and these features are invariable, only the Psalms, Hymn and *Capitulum* being changed in the several forms of the office.

The Psalter contains, as we have said, the " Common of Time." The " Proper of Time," or *Temporale*, adds the variations of the weekly round occasioned by the seasons of the Christian year. To some extent changes of this nature are familiar to English Churchmen, for the principle is recognised in our present Prayer Book; the daily Order, for example, is broken by the change once a week at least of the " Collect for the Day"; on Easter Day the *Venite* gives place to the " Easter Anthems," and for every day in the year there are appointed either daily or " proper" Lessons. But these departures from the usual order are slight indeed when compared with those which were necessary under the old system. Every Sunday throughout the year and nearly every weekday brought its own contribution, not merely of lessons and collects, but of hymns, antiphons, responds, *capitula*. The Lessons however formed the bulk of the *Temporale*; as we have seen, they had no place in the Psalter, and the daily lessons of the whole year had to be sought in the "Proper of Time." Under our present system a kalendar suffices, but where the lessons were taken not only from Holy Scripture but from the Fathers and the lives of the saints and acts of the martyrs, it was impossible to escape from the necessity of copying them in full into the great Church Breviaries.

The complications introduced by the "Proper of Time" were increased by the "Common" and "Proper of Saints." These two sections of the Breviary supplied the offices proper to the fixed non-Dominical holy days. The "Common of Saints" provided those which belonged equally to a whole class of saints, e.g. apostles or martyrs or virgins; the "Proper of Saints," those which were peculiar to a particular saint.

In the attempt to work into a connected whole the materials to be drawn from these four sources, the mediaeval clergy were assisted by two other portions of the Breviary,

THE BREVIARY. 65

the Kalendar and the *Ordinale*. The kalendar of the Breviary was in the main a list of the fixed festivals written against the days of the year on which they fell. Beside the fixed Dominical holy days, the Nativity, Circumcision, and Epiphany, and the days sacred to the saints of the New Testament, it contained also the festivals of a large but uncertain number of ecclesiastical saints. Local influences determined the addition or omission of many of these names from the kalendar, just as they determined the addition or omission of commemorations in the "Proper of Saints." As soon as the saint had been recognized, his name was added to the local kalendar; and by consulting the kalendar the priest could see at a glance on what day his festival was to be observed. Further, the kalendar was usually accompanied by calculations which enabled him to discover the incidence of the movable feasts, such as are still given after the tables of lessons in our Book of Common Prayer.

Yet the kalendar alone carried the priest but a little way. Indeed, his difficulties began when he had learnt from it the name of the saint or saints to be commemorated on a particular day. As one of the days of the

E

week, the Saint's Day was provided with a service in the Psalter; as one of the days of the ecclesiastical year, a further provision was made for it in the *Temporale*; and now the *Sanctorale* came in to add to his perplexity. Moreover, there might be conflicting claims to reconcile, as for instance when a Saint's Day coincided with a great Sunday or Dominical holy day. But here again the Breviary supplied the desired guidance. The *Ordinale* taught the clergy how to regulate " the relative precedence to be given to Sunday, Saint's Day, Commemoration, and weekday services." It consisted of tables arranged according to the Sunday letters, and presenting every possible combination of services [1]. In the printed edition of the Sarum Breviary the *Ordinale*, or, as it is also called, the *Pica Sarum*, or, in English, the "Pie," is broken up into sections which are inserted in the Temporale at certain intervals. At the end of the fifteenth century the clergy had a more convenient guide to the Breviary services in the *Directorium Sacerdotum* of Clement Maydeston; but the "Pie" retained its place

[1] See P. and W. ii. p. xii, and for a further account, iii. p. lxiii ff. Also C. Wordsworth, *Tracts of C. Maydeston* (Introduction).

in the printed Breviaries. A glance at the Cambridge edition of the Sarum Breviary[1] will enable the reader to judge for himself whether Cranmer was justified in his criticism: "the number and hardness of the rules called the *Pie*, and the manifold changings of the Service was the cause, that to turn the Book only was so hard and intricate a matter, that many times there was more business to find out what should be read, than to read it when it was found out."

The need of reform had long been felt on the Continent, and a radical revision of the Roman Breviary was attempted some years before the appearance of the English Order for Mattins and Evensong. The Spaniard, Fernandez de Quiñones, commonly known as Cardinal Quignon, General of the Franciscan Order in Spain, and the trusted friend of Popes Clement VII and Paul III, was the author of this reformed Breviary[2]; and so large was the demand for the work that it was reprinted six times between February, 1535, and July, 1536, and the second edition was issued from the press some twenty times

---

[1] E. g. P. and W., i. p. i, &c.
[2] Neale *Essays*, p. 3 f., and Dr. J. Wickham Legg's preface to the Cambridge reprint of Quignon's work (1888).

before its final withdrawal in 1566. Yet, in the first edition at least, the mediaeval services were revolutionized. The whole system of antiphons, responds, *capitula*, the entire musical setting of the offices which from the eighth century had been the pride of the Roman Church, was swept away at a stroke. Even the weekly recitation of the Psalter at Mattins and Vespers disappeared, and three fixed Psalms were attached to each office of the Hours. The lessons of Mattins were reduced to three, one from each Testament, the third taken from the Acts or Epistles, or if it was a Saint's Day, a reading from the life of the saint. The number of Saints' Days was largely diminished, and the *Temporale* or *Sanctorale* were brought within limits which to the adherents of the old order must have appeared meagre indeed.

That Cranmer not only knew Quignon's work, but was to some extent influenced by it, must be obvious to any one who has been at the pains to compare the preface in which the Spanish cardinal dedicated the revised Breviary to Paul III with that which the English Reformers prefixed to their first Book of Common Prayer. The English preface, still printed in our Prayer Books under the sub-title *Concerning the Service of the Church*, is largely indebted to Quignon, and in places is almost a translation of his address to the Pope [1]. Nevertheless, the first English Order for Daily Prayer is very far from being a servile imitation of Quignon's revision. Cranmer's purpose differed fundamentally from Quignon's; he desired to produce not merely a good manual of devotions for the clergy, but a Book of Common Prayer. The design developed itself in his mind very gradually. In 1542 the Sarum Breviary was made obligatory on the whole province of Canterbury—a first step towards uniformity. In the same year it was ordered that "the Curate of every Church, after the *Te Deum* and *Magnificat*, shall openly read unto the people one chapter of the New Testament in English, and when the New Testament is read over, then to begin the Old"—a first step towards the use of the vernacular. The next year the Archbishop brought down to Convocation a Royal message in favour of the reform of the Service-books, in which the 'portasses' were mentioned by name. On receiving this, Convocation proceeded to appoint two

---

[1] Palmer, *Origines Liturgicae*, i. p. 229 ff.

bishops, with six assessors from the Lower House, to inquire and report. Nothing more is heard of this committee till after the death of Henry, when one of the first acts of the clergy was to move for a report of the results at which it had arrived. But in the interval Cranmer at least had not been idle. Two MS. schemes for the reform of the daily offices have been lately brought to light, which show how the conception had grown in the Archbishop's mind. The first of these schemes " follows the old order of Breviary Services, and may be described as Sarum material worked up under Quignon influence. The second comes nearer to the form of Morning and Evening Prayer in the first printed Prayer Book of Edward VI... The preface of this latter scheme is manifestly an earlier draft of the English preface of the Book of 1549." With regard to details, the earlier scheme provides for all the Hours, while the latter retains only Mattins and Vespers, with a monthly recitation of the Psalms, and the reading of Scriptural lessons in English. The discovery of these documents is of considerable importance, because it shows how Cranmer, who was largely concerned in the final issue of the English

Prayer Book, felt his way from point to point, neither blindly following earlier reformers, whether Roman or Lutheran, nor on the other hand despising their help where it served the purpose he had in view[1].

When the new Order was at length matured and given to the world, it contained little which was not in the Sarum Breviary. The genius of Cranmer was shown not so much in creating new materials as in rearranging, compressing, and popularizing services which in their mediaeval form were adapted only for monastic or clerical use. The Hours were reduced to two, but the two were those which in the earliest times had alone been marked by assemblies for common psalmody and prayer. Moreover, the two offices retained by the English Church represented in their contents five out of the eight mediaeval offices. The new Order for Mattins was in fact a compression of the Sarum Mattins, Lauds, and Prime, the new Evensong included materials selected from Vespers and Compline; only the Apostolic Hours, which before the days of monasticism had been left to private devotion, were not represented in

---

[1] Gasquet and Bishop, *Edward VI and the B. of C. P.*, p. 16 f.; cf. the Appendices.

the English Book of Common Prayer. The following table will make this clear.

English Mattins.

Lord's Prayer Versicles, *Gloria* (Alleluia) *Venite* Psalms, with Gloria Lesson from O. T. *Te Deum*	From Sarum Mattins.
Lesson from N. T. Benedictus	From Sarum Lauds.
Kyrie Creed Lord's Prayer	From Sarum Prime.
Preces Collect of the day Collect for peace	From Sarum Lauds.
Collect for grace	From Sarum Prime.

English Evensong.

Lord's Prayer Versicles, *Gloria* (Alleluia) Psalms, with Gloria Lesson from O. T. Magnificat	From Sarum Evensong.
Lesson from N. T. Nunc Dimittis	From Sarum Compline.
Kyrie Creed Lord's Prayer Preces Collect of the day Collect for peace	From Sarum Evensong.
Collect for aid	From Sarum Compline.

THE BREVIARY. 73

Subsequent revisions of the Prayer Book have introduced into the English Mattins and Evensong elements foreign to the ancient Hours. Under this head we must place the Exhortation, Confession, and Absolution, prefixed to Morning Prayer in 1552; the supplementary Prayers for the Sovereign and the Royal Family, for the Clergy and People, with the Prayer of St. Chrysostom, finally added in 1662; lastly, the special Prayers and Thanksgivings, mostly of the Caroline period. The permission to use certain alternative canticles from the Old Testament in place of the Gospel canticles at Mattins and Evensong, is another departure from Sarum mediaeval practice, although ancient precedent is not wanting for the use of Old Testament canticles in other offices. But while the daily services have received, since 1549, many accessions from non-Sarum sources with one partial exception they have lost no ancient element which they then possessed. The exception is the *Alleluia* ordered by the first Prayer Book to be said near the beginning of Mattins and Evensong from Easter to Trinity Sunday. It disappeared in 1552, but in its place there has since been heard throughout the year the English response, "The Lord's Name be praised."

CHAPTER III.

THE MISSAL.

The *Liber Missalis*, *Missale*, or Missal, contained the service known to the Western Church as the *missa*, and by our Anglo-Saxon forefathers called "mæsse," the Mass [1]. *Missa*, another form of the Latin word *missio*, had been applied to the Eucharistic Office before the end of the fourth century. On the Palm Sunday of the year 385, Ambrose, Bishop of Milan, was disturbed at church by tidings of an Arian rising. He describes the incident in a letter to his sister, and adds, "But I stood firm at my post, and began to celebrate mass (*missam facere coepi*) [2]." The word means simply "dismissal." "In churches, palaces, and law-courts," writes Avitus of Vienne at the end of the fifth century, "the people are discharged from their attendance by the proclamation *missa fit*, "you are dis-

---

[1] Skeat, *Principles of English Etymology*, i. p. 436. See also Notes, p. 214.   [2] *Ep.* 20.

THE MISSAL.

missed[1]." In the Eucharistic service there were anciently two *missae*, or dismissals; the catechumens were sent away after the sermon, the baptized, if in full communion with the Church, remained till the end of the liturgy, and were then dismissed in the words which still stand at the end of the Roman Mass, *Ite, missa est.* "After the sermon," Augustine preaches[2], "the catechumens receive their dismissal (*missa fit catechumenis*); the faithful will stay." Hence the two portions of the service acquired the names of *missa catechumenorum* and *missa fidelium*, while the service as a whole was popularly spoken of as *missae, solemnia missarum*, or simply *missa.* The word was used occasionally of other services; thus in connexion with a monastic community we read of *vigiliarum missa*[3], *psalmorum missae*, and the like; but the Eucharist being the only public service ordinarily attended by the laity, it was natural that it should in the end acquire an exclusive right to a term which had come to mean an assembly gathered for religious worship.

The Eucharist was instituted at a social but sacred meal. The Passover meal was

[1] *Ep.* I.
[2] *Serm.* 49 § 8.
[3] E.g. Cassian, *Instit.* iii. 8. Cf. Du Cange, s. v. *missa.*

a feast upon a sacrifice, and as such it was regulated by a ritual based partly on the Mosaic law, partly on custom. The law of the Passover prescribed the eating of a cake of unleavened bread; custom had added the filling and drinking of cups of wine mingled with water. Other Paschal ceremonies were the solemn blessing and elevation of the Cup, a ceremonial washing of hands, and after the meal the recitation of "the great Hallel" (Pss. cxv–cxviii). At what exact point or points in the ritual of the Passover, the Eucharist was instituted cannot be determined beyond doubt from the narratives of the Synoptists and of St. Paul. The true text of St. Luke seems to place the Cup first[1]; whereas St. Paul distinctly states that the Cup was consecrated "after supper." But for our present purpose it is sufficient to realize that the new institution was grafted upon a social meal, which was at the same time a religious act, connected with a definite ritual and with certain liturgical forms[2].

From the first it was understood by the

---

[1] See Westcott and Hort, *Notes on Select Readings*, p. 63 f.
[2] For a full discussion of the connexion between the ceremonies of the Passover and the Eucharist, see Bickell, *Missa u. Pascha*, or Skene, *Passover Ritual*. The subject is discussed in a more popular manner in the *Dawn of Day* for 1896 (S. P. C. K.).

Church that the Eucharist was not intended to be merely an annual commemoration like the Passover, and the Apostolic Church celebrated it on the first day of every week or even daily [1]. It was therefore at once detached from the Passover, but for a generation or two the custom continued of connecting it with a social meal of another kind. Once a day or once a week the Christian brotherhood met at a common repast, the "Agape," so named after the new Christian virtue which bound them together in one; and their love-feast culminated in the solemn act which the Lord had commanded to be done as His memorial. But no sooner had the Church taken root in Gentile soil than the common meal was found to be a source of danger. St. Paul describes the excesses by which it was desecrated at Corinth, and the picture which St. Jude draws is still more discouraging [2]. The *agape* seems nevertheless to have maintained its connexion with the Eucharist in the early years of the second century, for Ignatius of Antioch tells the Church of Smyrna that "it is not permissible apart from the bishop either to baptize or to hold an

---

[1] Acts ii. 46; xx. 7.
[2] Jude 12; cf. 2 Pet. ii. 13.

agape (ἀγάπην ποιεῖν)," where the juxtaposition of baptism and the *agape* has been rightly taken to show that the Eucharist was still included in the latter[1]. The liturgical forms in the *Didache*[2] are most naturally explained on the same hypothesis; they are as follows:

"As touching the Eucharist, we give thanks on this wise. First for the Cup: 'We thank Thee, our Father, for the holy Vine of Thy servant David, which Thou didst make known to us through Thy Servant Jesus; to Thee be glory for ever.' And for the broken Bread: 'We thank Thee, our Father, for the life and knowledge which Thou didst make known to us through Thy Servant Jesus; to Thee be glory for ever. As this broken bread was once scattered upon the mountains, and being gathered together became one, so let Thy Church be gathered together from the ends of the earth into Thy kingdom; for Thine is the glory and the power through Jesus Christ for ever...' After the meal (μετὰ δὲ τὸ ἐμπλησθῆναι), give thanks on this wise: 'We give thanks to Thee, Holy Father, for thy Holy Name which Thou didst make to dwell in our hearts, and for the knowledge, faith, and immortality made known to us through Thy

---

[1] *Ep. ad Smyrn.* 8 (see Bp. Lightfoot's) note.
[2] C. 10, cf. cc. 14, 15 (Notes, p. 214 f.).

Servant Jesus; to thee be glory for ever. Thou, Almighty Lord, didst create all things for Thy Name's sake; Thou didst bestow food and drink upon men to enjoy, that they might give Thee thanks, and to us Thou didst grant spiritual food and drink and eternal life through Thy Servant. Before all things we give Thee thanks that Thou art mighty; to Thee be the glory for ever. Remember, Lord, Thy Church, to save it from all evil, and to perfect it in Thy love; and gather it from the four winds—that Church which was sanctified for Thy kingdom, which Thou didst prepare for it; for Thine is the power and the glory for ever.' 'Let grace come, and this world pass away.' 'Hosanna to the GOD of David.' 'If any be holy, let him come; if any be not, let him repent.' 'Maranatha. Amen.'"

These forms have been given at length both on account of their intrinsic interest, and because they are our earliest models of Eucharistic worship. But it is difficult to bring them into connexion with any known liturgy. Perhaps we shall not err if we see in the first and second of the three the blessing of the *agape* or common meal, and place the actual commemoration of the Lord's Death after the third. The words of institution are wanting, but for these the memory could be trusted, and they were perhaps felt to be too sacred to be committed to writing. In the short formulae that follow the last thanksgiving, we find distinct anticipations of later liturgical language; the proclamation, "If any be holy, let him come," anticipates the *sancta sanctis* of the liturgies, and warns us that the *agape* is over, and the communion of the Lord's Body and Blood is about to begin.

The forms in the *Didache* are provided for the use of the local bishops and deacons; the "prophets," it is expressly directed, are to be left free to use their own discretion as to the length of the Eucharistic prayer. There is reason to think that in the larger Christian societies, where the officers were men of education, this liberty was enjoyed by the local clergy also. The Epistle of Clement, which emanated from the Roman Church in the reign of Domitian, contains in its newly recovered part a prayer which runs through three chapters [1], and which has been shown by Bishop Lightfoot to be full of reminiscences of the prayers of the synagogue and temple, and of coincidences with the phraseology of the Christian liturgies. It is scarcely

[1] Cc. 59-61.

doubtful that this prayer is an echo of the Eucharistic worship of the Roman Church at the end of the first century [1]. Clement writes here much as he was accustomed to pray at the weekly Eucharist. Left free to lead the Eucharistic service of the Church in such words as he saw fit, his thoughts naturally took shape after the Jewish models to which the Apostolic Church had been accustomed; and the standard which he raised largely influenced the practice of his successors in the Roman See.

Fifty years after the date of Clement's letter an apology presented to Antoninus Pius (138–161) by Justin, a native of Palestine who had made his way to Rome, sketches for us the order of the Eucharistic service as it was celebrated at Rome in the middle of the second century. On Sunday, Justin says, all the Christians of a neighbourhood flocked from town and country to the place of assembly. The service began with the reading of the Gospels or of the Prophets, the length of the reading depending on the available time ($\mu \epsilon \chi \rho \iota \varsigma \, \epsilon \gamma \chi \omega \rho \epsilon \hat{\iota}$). Then the president (ὁ προεστώς, distinguished from the reader, ὁ ἀναγινώσκων) discoursed upon the lesson, after

---

[1] Lightfoot, *Clement*, i. p. 382 ff.

which the whole assembly rose and prayed. The prayers concluded, bread, wine, and water were brought to the president, who offered prayers and thanksgivings to the best of his ability (ὅση δύναμις αὐτῷ), the people responding 'Amen' (ὁ λαὸς ἐπευφημεῖ λέγων τὸ ἀμήν)[1]. Then follows the distribution of the Eucharist, which is effected by the deacons, who after the service carry portions to the absent. A collection is made for the sick and needy, but whether during the service, and if so at what point in it, Justin does not say[2]. It will be gathered from this picture that while the long Eucharistic prayer was still left to the discretion of the bishop, the Eucharist in Justin's time had ceased to be connected with a social meal and had acquired a fixed and stately order. The reader will have noticed the general agreement of this order with our own; the Gospel, the sermon, the prayers for the faithful, the Eucharistic or Consecration prayer, the communion of the faithful, are all features common to the Roman Eucharist of the second century and the present Anglican service.

The Roman liturgy was still, doubtless,

---

[1] Cf. 1 Cor. xiv. 16.
[2] Justin, *Apol.* i. c. 65, 67 (Notes, p. 215 f.).

Greek in language and in its general tone. Of the Latin liturgy, as of the Latin Bible, the first traces are to be found in the Church of North Africa. The Church of Carthage had drawn her liturgical order, together with her Christianity, from Rome, and traces of the service may be seen in the earliest literature of African Christianity. In the Acts of Perpetua and Felicitas (c. A.D. 202) the martyr Saturus describes a vision in which the joys of Paradise are revealed to him: "We heard," he says, "the voices of those who said with one accord and without ceasing, 'Agios, Agios, Agios[1].'" That we have here a liturgical formula is nearly certain, both from the use of the Greek words in a Latin text, and from the words "without ceasing" (*sine cessatione, ἀκαταπαύστως*), which occur in the liturgies immediately before the *Ter Sanctus*. Half a century later Cyprian refers to the preface by which the *Ter Sanctus* is still preceded in all liturgies: "before the Prayer, the priest recites a preface wherein he prepares the minds of the faithful, saying, 'Lift up your hearts'; and the people answer, 'We lift them up unto the Lord,' being thus admonished that they must fix their thoughts

[1] *Texts and Studies*, i. 2. p. 80.

upon the Lord alone [1]." The same forms were used at Rome in the third century, if we may accept the evidence of the Hippolytean canons [2].

When we pass to the fourth century, these scraps of information are supplemented by full accounts of the Eucharistic service and the earliest complete liturgy. But the light comes at first chiefly from the East, from Jerusalem and Antioch, rather than from Rome.

We will begin with the witness of a well-known ecclesiastic, which can be dated. Cyril, Presbyter and afterwards Bishop of Jerusalem, delivered to those who had been newly baptized at the Easter of the year 347 a lecture—the last of his five 'Mystagogic Catecheses'—in which he describes and comments upon the liturgy of his own Church. You have seen, he begins, the deacon offer the celebrant and the priests who surround the altar, water to wash their hands. This is a symbolic act to be interpreted by Ps. xxvi. 6, "I will wash my hands in innocency, and so will I go to Thine altar." Then the deacon proclaims, "Let us greet one another," and the "holy kiss" is exchanged. After this the celebrant begins: "Lift up your

[1] *De Orat. Dom.* 31.   [2] Achelis, p. 50 f.

hearts (ἄνω τὰs καρδίας)," and the preface and *Ter Sanctus* follow. Then comes an invocation of the Holy Spirit: "we pray God of His love to send forth the Holy Ghost upon the gifts (τὰ προκείμενα), that He may make the bread the Body of Christ and the wine His Blood." Intercession succeeds : and the sacrifice being now consummated, the Church supplicates God for the world, for kings and their armies, for the sick and all who need His help. Mention is made of the departed, especially of the fathers and bishops of the Church. The whole is concluded by the Lord's Prayer, the people answering "Amen." Then the priest proclaims, "Holy things for the holy," and they respond, "There is One Holy, One Lord, Jesus Christ." Ps. xxxiv. 9 ("O taste and see," &c.) is sung, and the communicants approach, extending the right hand supported by the left to receive the Bread ; the Cup is then administered, and when all have partaken, a prayer completes the service [1].

Addressing the newly baptized, Cyril had no occasion to describe the earlier part of the liturgy, with which they had been familiar during their catechumenate. But what it

[1] *C. M.* v. (Notes, p. 216).

was in Syria in the fourth century we can learn from the second book of the *Apostolical Constitutions* [1]. There we are introduced into a church at the moment when the liturgy is about to begin and are bidden to observe the entire order of service. The "House of Prayer," as it is called, is an oblong building, with three apses at the eastern end. In the central apse is the bishop's throne; the presbyters sit upon either hand, the deacons stand near; the nave is filled with the faithful, the men on one side, the women on the other. Then the reader mounts a platform and reads a lesson from the Old Testament, the precentor at intervals chanting Psalms, in which the people join at certain points. Readings from the Acts and Epistles follow, after which the Gospel is read by the deacon or presbyter, the whole congregation standing. After the Gospel, exhortations are given by the presbyters in turn (ὁ καθεὶς αὐτῶν), and by the bishop [2]. The catechumens and penitents are then dismissed; the deacon proclaims, "Let none remain who is at enmity or a dissembler" (μήτις κατά τινος, μήτις ἐν ὑποκρίσει), and the

---

[1] C. 57.
[2] A practice borrowed from the synagogue; cf. Acts xiii. 15; cf. 1 Cor. xiv. 13.

second part of the service, the *missa fidelium*, begins.

This is a mere outline; but the eighth book of the *Constitutions* contains a complete liturgy [1]. Unhappily this earliest written liturgy cannot be regarded as precisely reflecting the Use of any Church. Indeed it does not profess to do so; it is clearly an ideal, based no doubt upon the practice of the Church to which the writer belonged, but not in any way tied to the precise forms which were current [2]. Yet we may be sure that the writer has not departed widely from the general order of the accustomed service, his purpose being to claim Apostolic authority for an existing scheme. Moreover, we recognize in this imaginary Apostolic liturgy features with which we are familiar through the *Catecheses* of Cyril and the second book of the *Constitutions*. First there is the reading of the Law and Prophets, the Epistles, Acts, and Gospels; then the sermon; then follow lengthy and separate dismissals of catechumens, energumens, *competentes* (candidates for baptism in the final stage of preparation), and penitents. Then—a new feature—a long bidding prayer

---

[1] C. 5 seq. [2] See Brightman, *Liturgies* (1896), i. p. xliii.

is said by the deacon, the people responding to each invitation, *Kyrie eleison*; after which the bishop offers a prayer for the faithful. The kiss of peace and the washing of the priest's hands follow; then the deacon warns the disqualified or unworthy not to approach. After this the gifts are solemnly offered; and the bishop begins the *anaphora* with the Apostolic benediction, followed immediately by *Sursum corda*. The remainder of the service differs but slightly, in point of order, from that which is described by Cyril.

The reader, however slight his acquaintance with the subject, will not have failed to notice in all these glimpses of ancient Eucharistic worship a uniform plan, unfolding itself gradually and with some diversity of detail during the interval between Justin and Cyril. In those two centuries the ceremonial of the Eucharist had undoubtedly developed, and the minor features of the service had assumed a more definite order and form; but there is no essential change of scheme. The lessons and sermon, the earlier prayers, the great Eucharistic prayer ending with the people's "Amen," the communion in both kinds—all these elements are common to every stage of liturgical development, from the second century to the fourth. Some of the liturgical forms, too, were evidently common to Churches the most remote in locality and general character; the *Sursum corda* with its sequel has met us in the Latin Church of North Africa as well as in the Churches of Syria. On the other hand the liberty enjoyed by the "prophets" in the communities referred to by the *Didache*, and by the earlier bishops in other Churches, of using their discretion as to the precise words of the Thanksgiving, must naturally have led to many types of liturgical worship, and even to variations in the order of the service. It might have been supposed that under these conditions every Church would in time possess a liturgy of its own, modelled after the customs and devotional peculiarities of its great bishops. But this tendency to an excessive multiplication of liturgical types was corrected by another circumstance—the commanding influence which certain Churches acquired even at an early date. Such influence was usually though not exclusively due to the connexion of these Churches with the great cities of the Empire. Thus the sixth canon of Nicaea (325) recognizes the ancient jurisdiction of the Bishop of Alexandria over Egypt, Libya, and Pentapolis, and of the Bishop of Rome over the "suburbicarian" Churches of Italy; Antioch is also mentioned as possessing certain privileges which are less clearly defined[1]. In North Africa, the Bishop of Carthage was regarded as primate; in Palestine, while Caesarea was the metropolitan city, Jerusalem was accorded an honorary precedence; in the further east, Edessa was supreme. At a later time Constantinople, in her capacity of "New Rome," claimed a dignity only second to that of the older seat of empire. Westwards, Milan was in the fourth century almost a rival of Rome; Arles took the lead in Gaul, and Toledo in Spain. To some of these great Churches belonged the still higher honour of a real or supposed connexion with an apostle or evangelist; Jerusalem could claim St. James, Alexandria St. Mark, Rome St. Peter, whilst far-off Edessa regarded St. Thaddaeus as its founder[2].

It is easy to see how the pre-eminence of certain Churches gave wider circulation to the types of Eucharistic service which had become traditional with them. Thus the liturgical influence of Alexandria was felt throughout Egypt and Abyssinia; Western

---

[1] Bright, *Councils*, pp. 20, 27.   [2] Cf. *Origines*, c. 1.

Syria was dominated by Caesarea and Antioch, Eastern Syria by Edessa; Constantinople, which drew its inspiration from Antioch, eventually imposed the Antiochian type upon the Orthodox East. In the West, North Africa followed a liturgy essentially identical with that which is now known as the Roman Mass; Milan, Arles, Toledo, each had its own liturgical peculiarities, together with certain common characteristics which distinguished the Gallican and Spanish services from Eastern liturgies on the one hand and from the Roman Mass on the other. Five great liturgical families ultimately divided between them the Christian world: the West and East Syrian, the Alexandrian, the Roman and the Gallican. The last two alone concern us directly, as the only families known to the West, and as having both found a place in the liturgical history of these islands.

Of the Gallican type of liturgy little need be said. Unfortunately, no complete Mass of a purely Gallican character has survived; we have to reconstruct the order of service from scraps of mutilated Service-books [1], and from the casual notices of Gallican writers such as Sulpicius Severus, Caesarius of Arles,

[1] See a specimen in the Notes, p. 217.

and Gregory of Tours, and the analogy of the Mozarabic liturgy which is near of kin, although of independent growth. Still we have materials enough to determine its general character. It is distinguished from all Eastern liturgies by the large proportion of variable forms which it possesses. On the other hand it has many clear traces of Eastern influence which are wanting in the Roman Mass. Two remarkable features, which distinguish the Gallican rite from all others, are the frequent occurrence in the service of short prayers called *collectiones*, and the use of a hortatory or explanatory introduction, varying with the occasion and known as the *praefatio missae*; what is called the "Preface" in liturgies of the Roman type is in Gallican fragments and writers known as the *contestatio* or *immolatio*. The origin of this liturgical family is still obscure. M. Duchesne thinks that it may be traced to the great Church of Milan, which still possesses a liturgy of its own, showing Eastern influence and some affinity to the Gallican type[1]. But this parentage has not been decisively established, and the Ambrosian Mass, as we know

---

[1] *Origines*, p. 84 ff. On the other hand, cf. Ceriani, *Notitia Liturgiae Ambrosianae*, esp. p. 81.

it, is certainly far nearer to the Roman than to the early liturgies of Gaul.

To the Roman Mass let us now come. We have referred to the liturgical language at the end of Clement's letter, but these Greek devotions have little in common with the essentially Latin tone of the later "Canon of the Mass." The Roman Church, to which St. Paul wrote in Greek, continued to be a Greek-speaking community for at least another century. The Shepherd of Hermas, as well as the Epistle of Clement, was written in Greek, "indeed all the literature that we can in any way connect with Christian Rome down to the end of the reign of M. Aurelius is Greek[1]." Victor, who became Bishop of Rome in 189, was "apparently the first Latin prelate who held the metropolitan see of Latin Christendom[2]," and Victor, if we can trust the *Liber Pontificalis*, was not a Roman but an African Christian. In Africa, as we have seen, the liturgy was probably Latin almost from the first, for Greek was understood at Carthage only by the educated. Was it Victor who introduced the use of a Latin service at Rome? We are left to

---

[1] Sanday and Headlam's *Romans*, p. lii. f.
[2] Lightfoot, *Philippians*, p. 221.

conjecture. But the forms preserved in the canons of Hippolytus seem to have been Greek[1], at least in the more solemn parts of the Mass. Indeed, the earliest trace in literature of a Latin Mass connected with the Church of Rome occurs in a letter which is attributed to Pope Innocent I (401-418). It is addressed to the Umbrian Bishop Decentius, and asserts the right of the Roman see to impose upon the other Western Churches the customs of the Church of Rome; and among these is mentioned the giving of the *Pax* or Kiss of Peace after the Lord's Prayer of the Canon. Now we know from one of the sermons of St. Augustine[2] that this was the place of the *Pax* in the Mass of North Africa, whilst it is certainly not a feature of any existing liturgy except those which belong to the Roman family. This circumstance points to the affinity of the Roman Mass with that of the African Church; and it shows beyond doubt that at the beginning of the fifth century Rome possessed, and probably had possessed for a considerable time, an order of service marked by one of the distinctive characteristics of her present Use. On the other hand it reveals a reluctance on

---

[1] Achelis, p. 50 f. [2] *Serm.* 227.

the part even of neighbouring Churches to abandon their own ritual in favour of the ritual of Rome. It appears that an Umbrian town, not a hundred miles from Rome, situated in one of the *regiones suburbicariae*, and therefore within the direct jurisdiction of the Pope, had hitherto contrived to maintain its own Use. Innocent's endeavour to restrain its freedom was the first of a series of aggressions which have succeeded in stamping out, with rare exceptions, the non-Roman forms of the Western liturgy.

Three great successors of Innocent are connected in the popular belief with the development of the Roman Mass, Leo I (†461), Gelasius (†496), and Gregory I (†604). Leo is said by his biographer, Anastasius Bibliothecarius, to have added a few words to the Canon; according to Gennadius, Gelasius wrote a treatise on the Sacraments (*Tractatus Sacramentorum*), whilst the *Liber Pontificalis* attributes to him the composition of collects and prefaces[1]; Gregory, as we know from his own writings, inserted a paragraph in the Canon, and placed the Lord's Prayer, after the example of the Greek liturgies, at the end of the Prayer of Consecration[2].

[1] i. p. 255.   [2] Duchesne, *Origines*, pp. 168, 176.

If we may believe his biographer, John the Deacon, Gregory's liturgical labours went much further; he revised the work of Gelasius, "removing many things, changing a few, and adding some," and he "brought the whole within the limits of a single book" (*in unius libelli volumine coarctavit*). In the eighth and ninth centuries books were undoubtedly in circulation which bore the name of Gelasius and Gregory.

From the fourth century onwards we hear of liturgical books in Western Europe. Paulinus of Nola is credited by Gennadius with the composition of a Sacramentary (*fecit et sacramentarium*)[1]; Jerome ascribes a *liber mysteriorium* to Hilary of Poitiers[2]; Musaeus of Marseilles, and Voconius, a Mauritanian bishop, both compiled similar volumes about the year 460. There can be little doubt that such collections existed at Rome in the days of Leo and Gelasius, if not indeed in those of Innocent. But it is another matter to identify with them existing MSS. of Latin Sacramentaries. Since the sixteenth century particular types of the Sacramentary have been identified with the names of Leo, Gelasius, and Gregory respectively, and it has

---

[1] *De Vir. Illustr.* 48.   [2] *Ibid.* 100.

become the fashion to speak of their contents as "Leonian," "Gelasian," or "Gregorian." A closer examination has convinced liturgical scholars that this identification cannot be maintained, at least in the sense in which it is generally understood. The Leonian book, preserved in a MS. belonging to the Chapter of Verona, is indeed of purely Roman origin; but it is neither so early as Leo, nor does it represent the official services of the Roman Church. The MS. is of the seventh century, and the book cannot be older than the sixth, for it contains a collect for the anniversary of Pope Simplicius (†483), and refers to the siege of Rome by the Ostrogoths in A.D. 537-8; on the other hand it may be pre-Gregorian, and must in that case be placed before 590. That it was a Roman book is clear from numerous local allusions—references now to a basilica, now to a catacomb, where the Mass is to be said; that it was a collection made by some ecclesiastic for his own use, and not a normal Roman altar-book of the sixth century, may be inferred from the great number of alternative forms which it brings together, and from the absence of anything like an orderly arrangement of the materials.

The Gelasian Sacramentary is found in several MSS. Two of the three most important Gelasian MSS. mention "the kingdom of the Franks," and were evidently intended for use in Frankish territory. But the book is on the whole Roman and not Gallican, and may be taken fairly to represent the Roman Mass of its time. It is, however, post-Gregorian, for it contains Gregory's additions, and the Canon ends with the Lord's Prayer. The so-called Gregorian Sacramentary represents a still later revision of the Roman Mass, which at the end of the eighth century passed for the work of Gregory. At that time, " probably between 784 and 791 [1]," a copy of the Sacramentary, believed to be Gregory's, was sent by Pope Adrian I to Charlemagne, who had expressed the wish to circulate through his dominion the most correct form of the Roman service. The " Gregorian " books are based upon this official copy, as the " Gelasian " MSS. represent the unrevised Sacramentaries previously in use. But whilst these books contain the Roman Use of the end of the eighth century, they include a supplement which consists of non-Roman matter added by some eccle-

[1] Wilson, *Gelasian Sacramentary* (.894), p. liii f.

siastic of Charles's court, possibly by our countryman Alcuin. Thus neither the Gelasian nor the Gregorian books, as they now exist, can be used without considerable reserve as guides to the Roman Mass of the seventh and eighth centuries. In each case the basis is Roman, but the books have come to us through Frankish hands. Still, after all deductions, there is much to be learnt from these three types of the Roman Sacramentary. The "Leonian" enables us to carry back the origin of many of our finest collects to a date earlier than the sixth century; and its wealth of *missae*, i.e. variable portions of the Mass written for particular occasions, reveals the liturgical activity of the Roman Church in pre-Gregorian times. From the "Gelasian" Sacramentary, which has reached us nearly complete, we learn what were the contents of the altar-book in the seventh century. The book provides for the seasons, the Saints' Days, and the Sundays of the Church year. Included in this provision we find the ordination services of the Roman Church under Lent, and the baptismal and confirmation services under Easter Eve; and, at the end of all, the Canon in full [1],

---

[1] Wilson, pp. 22 ff., 78 ff., 234 ff.

a large collection of *missae* for special occasions, together with benedictions and other devotional forms. The Roman portion of the "Gregorian" Sacramentary gives us both Ordinary and Canon, followed by the variable portions of the Mass from Christmas Eve to the fourth week of Advent, i.e. throughout the year.

The *Liber Sacramentorum* or *Sacramentarium* was a very comprehensive collection, containing not only all the forms belonging to the Mass, but those employed in other sacramental rites which were connected more or less remotely with the celebration of the Eucharist. But in one respect it entirely fails to guide us to a reconstruction of the Roman service. It is destitute of rubrics; in the use of its forms the priest was left almost entirely to his own discretion or to custom. As early as the beginning of the eighth century a remedy was sought for the confusion and uncertainty which were thus produced. A Frankish *capitulum* of the year 742 requires every priest to make for his own use a *libellus ordinis*, i.e. a book of directions for the arrangement of the altar service, and to submit it to the judgement of his bishop [1].

[1] Baluz. *Capit. Regn. Franc.* i. 824.

About the same time similar *libelli* came into use at Rome. A collection of *ordines Romani* was published by Mabillon, and may be read in Migne's Latin Patrology[1]: the first of them refers to the Mass, but describes a Mass at which the Pope himself officiates, and not the ordinary ceremonial of the altar. But another *ordo* is appended which gives the order of the paschal Mass; and with the aid of these two documents and a treatise by Amalarius of Metz, who about 830 undertook a journey to Rome for the purpose of investigating the Roman practice, it is possible to form a fairly accurate conception of the Mass as it was performed in Rome at the beginning of the ninth century.

Besides the Sacramentary and the Ordo, the Roman priest of the eighth or ninth century needed other books for use at the altar. The Sacramentaries are silent as to the scriptural lessons, which nevertheless found a place in every liturgy, and must have been read at Rome from the first. They were contained in several distinct collections: the *Lectionarium* or *Epistolarium* gave the readings from the Old Testament and the Epistles; the *Evangeliarium*, the

[1] *T.* lxxviii.

liturgical Gospels. A third book known as the *Comes* or *Liber Comitis* (or, in a corrupt form peculiar to Spain, the *Liber Comicus*), enabled the priest to find the lections for the day[1]. Every great Church had its own lectionary and its own *comes*. The Roman *comes*, which was attributed to Jerome and called the *Comes Hieronymi*, has special interest for Englishmen, for this book continues to regulate the Epistles and Gospels of the Church of England; and it may be to our loyalty to the earlier Roman *comes* that we owe the divergence of some of our Eucharistic lections from those of the modern Roman Use.

Another necessary book was the *Antiphonarium*, or, as it seems to have been called at Rome, the *Cantatorium*; not identical with the Antiphonary of the Hour offices, but a collection of the musical portions of the Mass. St. Augustine speaks of a Psalm being sung in his time between the Epistle and the Gospel. For this, at a later time, was substituted an anthem consisting of a verse and response, afterwards known as the *graduale*

---

[1] Cf. G. Morin, *Anecd. Maredsol.*, vol. i, p. v. Du Cange, s. v. *comicus*.

—in English "grayle" or "grail." Antiphonaries containing these anthems for use at the mass are already mentioned among Roman Service-books in the ninth century, and like the revised Sacramentary, are attributed to Gregory. As time went on, the gradual assumed a more elaborate form. During the interval between Easter and Whitsuntide it was followed by Alleluia; at other times by the *tract*, a verse sung *tractim* (i. e. continuously) by the *cantor*. The last syllable of the Alleluia was protracted through a long musical passage; at a later time this monotonous prolongation was relieved by the introduction of a "prose" or a "sequence," a composition which supplied words to the music. Such "sequences" were numerous in the mediaeval mass; Sarum had ninety-four, York one hundred and seventy-two. In connexion with other musical insertions or "farsings" of the Mass, they sometimes formed a volume which was known as the "Troper" (*troperium* [1]). While the *graduale* contained the introits, and the offertory, communion anthems, and post-communions, as well as the grails, the Troper received the accessory words and

---

[1] On the Troper, see Frere, *Winchester Troper* (1894), Intr., p. vi ff.

music which custom had attached not only to these portions of the Mass, but to the *Gloria in Excelsis, Credo, Sanctus,* and *Agnus Dei.*

Such were the books which were needed at least for the solemn performance of the Mass, and which were digested into the mediaeval Missal. At first the name of missal—*liber missalis* or *missale*—was given to the Sacramentary, which contained the *missae* and the Canon of the Mass, as distinguished from the other books used at the altar. Thus when in the eighth century Egbert, Archbishop of York, spoke of Gregory's "missalis liber[1]" he meant without doubt the Sacramentary which at that time passed in England as the work of Gregory. Inventories written in the early part of the ninth century make mention both of Gregorian and Gelasian Missals, i.e. of the two recensions of the Roman Sacramentary then current in the Frankish empire. A capitulary of Lewis the Pious requires the bishops to see that the parish priests possess a Missal and a Lectionary; episcopal orders issued to the clergy of this same period call upon them to provide the necessary church books, among which are specified a Missal, a book of the

[1] Haddan and Stubbs, iii. p. 411.

Gospels and a Lectionary (i.e. an Epistolarium). Even the phrase *missale plenarium*, as occasionally used in the ninth century, appears to mean no more than a complete Sacramentary. The incorporation of the various books in a single MS. seems to have been a later conception: Muratori says that he knew of no complete missal, in the latter sense, earlier than the eleventh century. Even when the compendious Missal came into general use, it did not supersede the necessity of separate books for the Epistles and Gospels and for the musical portions of the Mass. The Missal, however, as fully developed, contained all that the parish priest needed as he stood at the altar to say Mass; it took the place of the Sacramentary and the *Ordo*, and to some extent rendered the priest independent of the other books when they could not easily be had.

Let us proceed to examine the contents of the Missal commonly used in England before the Reformation.

The distribution of the material of the Missal is analogous to that which we have observed in the Breviary, i.e. it contains the " Common " and " Proper of Time " and the

"Common" and "Proper of Saints." But whereas in the Breviary the Common of Time is represented by the Psalter, which is the backbone of the Hour services, in the Missal it consists of the Ordinary and Canon of the Mass, i.e. the framework which is common to every Mass, and into which all the special provisions of the *missae* must be fitted.

We begin with this framework, for though it does not stand in the forefront of the Missal, the other portions of the book are not intelligible until it has been mastered. It consists of two portions. The old division into *missa catechumenorum* and the *missa fidelium* has long disappeared, for there are no longer any adult catechumens to be dismissed before the more solemn part of the Mass begins. In place of it a distinction is now drawn between the absolutely invariable portion of the Mass, and that which precedes it and admits of variable elements. The former, known in the East as the *Anaphora*, and in the West as the *Canon*, consists of the solemn consecration and offering of the memorial sacrifice; the latter, known to Westerns as the *Ordinarium*, contains all that comes before the Canon, and into it were grafted the lections and devotions proper to the seasons and the holy days. The Canon may be regarded as the oldest part of the Roman Mass, and, with the exception of the new paragraph and the slight change of order due to Gregory, it has probably remained unaltered since the fifth or sixth centuries; if not indeed since the third or fourth. Pope Vigilius at any rate writes in A.D. 538: "With us the order of prayers at Mass is not varied by particular seasons or holy days; the gifts are always consecrated in the same words[1]." The Churches subject to Rome used the Roman Canon, whatever divergences might be tolerated in other parts of the Mass; and we cannot doubt that in this respect the Norman Church in England merely followed the practice of pre-Norman times, or that, excepting the period of Celtic influence in Northumbria, the Roman Canon was used in England from the days when Augustine sang his first Mass at St. Martin's, Canterbury.

Let us now follow the order of the Sarum service[2]. While vesting, the priest and his ministers said the hymn *Veni Creator* with

[1] *Ep. ad Profut.*
[2] *Missale ad Usum Sarum.* Burntisland, 1861.

the versicle and response, "Send forth thy Spirit and they shall be created. *R.* And Thou shalt renew the face of the earth," followed by the Collect for Purity (*Deus cui omne cor patet*, &c.). As they approached the altar Ps. xliii (*Judica me*) was said with the antiphon, "I will go unto the altar of God" (*introibo ad altare Dei*), and after the antiphon *Kyrie eleison* and *Pater noster*. Then came the confession and absolution of the priest and ministers; and the Psalm *Adiutorium nostrum*, after which the priest, deacon, and sub-deacon gave one another a kiss of peace (peculiar in this place to Sarum and Bangor), and the prayer *Aufer a nobis* was offered. Then followed *Gloria in Excelsis*, the collect (or collects) for the day, the Epistle and Gradual, the Gospel, the "Nicene" Creed, the *Offertorium* and prayer of oblation (*Suscipe sancta Trinitas*), the washing of the priest's hands, the "secret" prayers, the *Sursum corda*, preface, *Sanctus*, *Hosanna*. Of these elements of the ordinary the variable ones are the *Introit* (which the Sarum rubrics call *officium*) and the Psalm following, the Collect, Epistle, and Gospel, with the Gradual and its extensions, the *Offertorium*, the *Secreta* and the proper preface.

After the Hosanna the priest begins the Canon. Here, as we have said, the Sarum form is practically identical with the Roman, the only appreciable differences being in the rubrics. This venerable portion of the service consists of one long prayer, concluding with the *Pater noster*; but in MSS. and editions it is conventionally broken up into paragraphs, known to liturgiologists by their opening words (*Te igitur, memento Domine, communicantes, hanc igitur, quam oblationem, qui pridie, unde et memores, supra quae propitio, supplices te rogamus, memento etiam, nobis quoque*). These devotions fall under three heads—intercession, commemoration, and oblation; for a fourth feature which is prominent in Eastern *anaphorae* has no clear place in the Roman Canon, viz. the invocation of the Holy Spirit upon the elements. The Roman and Sarum Canon is further distinguished by its practice of separating the intercession for the living from that for the departed members of the Church, the former being placed before, the latter after the words of consecration.

After the Canon properly so called there followed, if a bishop were celebrant, a solemn benediction of the people. The *Pax* was then given and the *Agnus Dei* sung; then came the communion of the priest and people, the latter accompanied by the variable anthem known as *communio*, and followed by a prayer called *post-communio*. The whole was concluded by the deacon's proclamation *Ite, missa est*, or on certain occasions *Benedicamus Domino*. On his way back to the vestry the priest said the first fourteen verses of the Gospel according to St. John.

This account is necessarily meagre; no notice has been taken of the elaborate ritual, or of minor forms of devotion, such as those connected with the fraction of the host, and the commixture of the consecrated elements. Moreover, it must be remembered that the Ordinary and Canon occupy only a few leaves of the Missal, the bulk of the book being filled with the variable elements of the Mass, which had to be worked into the frame day after day by the officiating clergy. Let us turn to the "Proper of Time," and open at the First Sunday in Advent. The special features of the service of that day include Introit and Psalm, Collect, Epistle, and Gospel, Gradual and sequence, Offertory, Secrets, Communion anthem and post-Communion prayer. Besides this array of *propria* for the Sunday, a special Epistle and Gospel are given for the Monday,

Wednesday, and Friday in the following week. Similar provision is made week after week, though the week-day variables are more numerous at some seasons than at others; thus in Holy Week every day has them in full, whereas during the weeks after Trinity the Wednesdays alone are signalized in this way. The "Proper" and "Common of Saints" add largely, of course, to this richness of material; every holy day has its proper variables, and in certain cases, others are appointed for the octave or even for every day between the feast and its octave. Nor does this enumeration exhaust the contents of the Sarum Missal. There is a large collection of "votive" masses: a Mass of the Holy Trinity, of the Angels, of the Holy Ghost, of the Body of Christ; a Mass for sinners, for penitents, for the sick, for rain, in time of war, in time of plague. There are again the *memoriae communes*, as they were called, including special collects, &c., for all conditions of men and all the circumstances of life; e.g. for the Pope, for the King, for travellers, for peace, against evil thoughts, and so forth. Lastly, since marriage and burial were connected with the celebration of the Eucharist, the Missal contains offices for both.

Such was the altar-book which the English Reformers found firmly established in the affections both of the priesthood and laity; a book of which the central part could lay claim to a venerable antiquity, while the rest had grown up in the course of centuries, largely on English soil, as the expression of the deepest wants of the people, for which they had sought relief in the one service ordained by Christ Himself. The Missal undoubtedly needed revision, but the task of revising it must have been felt by Cranmer and his associates to be the most delicate and difficult of the liturgical problems which lay before them.

At first revision only was contemplated. "All Mass books," Convocation was told in 1543, were to be "newly examined, reformed, and castigated." Even after Henry's death (Jan. 28, 1547) the Archbishop proceeded with caution. His own mind does not seem to have been quite made up upon the preliminary question of the use of the Latin tongue. Those parts of the Mass which were concerned with the instruction of the laity or the guidance of their devotions might evidently be said with advantage in the vulgar tongue; and as early as August, 1547, an order was issued for the reading of the Epistle and Gospel in English at High Mass. On the same principle, when the young King attended Mass at the opening of his first Parliament in the following November, the *Gloria in Excelsis*, the Creed, and the *Agnus Dei* were sung in English. Meanwhile, the wider question was already under discussion. A paper had been circulated among the bishops containing the question, "Whether in the Mass it were convenient to use such speech as the people may understand?" Cranmer replied, "I think it convenient to have the vulgar tongue in the Mass, except in certain mysteries, whereof I doubt." It would seem as if up to this time the Archbishop might have been satisfied by a revised English version of the Sarum Mass, with some portions of the Canon left in the original Latin.

The next year a more serious step was taken. Before the end of 1547 both Houses of Parliament had passed an Act for the restoration of the Cup to the laity. This change rendered necessary a slight addition in that part of the service which regulated the communion of the laity, and the opportunity was taken of preparing a short English office both of preparation and communion. On March 8, 1548, an English *Order of Communion* was issued under royal authority, consisting of an Exhortation, General Confession and Absolution, the "Comfortable Words" and the Prayer of Humble Access, the words to be used at the "delivering of both kinds," and the final blessing. These forms were intended to serve as a temporary supplement to the Latin Mass, and to be used "without the varying of any other rite or ceremony in the Mass, until other order shall be provided."

To those who clung to the old service the words just quoted must have had an ominous sound. Occasion was soon found for the "other order" to which they seemed to point. The clergy did not render uniform obedience to the provisional order. Some used only a part of it, others ignored it altogether. Matters were thus precipitated, and during the summer of 1548 the question of "enforcing uniformity" was anxiously considered. It appears that a committee of the bishops sat from time to time at Windsor to prepare forms of service for use both in choir and at the altar. In January, 1549, the first Act of Uniformity was passed, and appended to it was the first English Book of Common Prayer.

The new book contained, amongst other forms, "The Supper of the Lord and the Holy Communion, commonly called the Mass," preceded by "the Introits, Collects, Epistles, and Gospels to be used at the celebration of the Lord's Supper and Holy Communion through the year." The "Supper of the Lord and the Holy Communion" corresponded to the Ordinary and Canon of the Mass, with the insertion of the new "Order of Communion," which was now permanently added; the "Introits, Collects, Epistles, and Gospels," provided the variables hitherto found under the "Proper of Time" and "of Saints."

It will be interesting to compare the English Ordinary and Canon with their predecessors. The new Ordinary contains the Lord's Prayer, Collect for Purity, Introit, Kyrie, Gloria in Excelsis, Collect for the King, Collect for the Day, Epistle and Gospel, Creed, Sermon or Homily, Offertory, Sursum Corda, Preface, Sanctus, Hosanna. If the reader will take the trouble to compare this list with the contents of the Sarum Ordinary, already given, he will see that the changes are not of great moment. The Confession and Absolution do not appear at this point in the English service, but they are merely postponed, finding a place further on in the preparation for the Communion of the People; the Gradual with its sequence has been removed—a change which was perhaps deliberate, since it is ordered that the Gospel shall follow "immediately after the Epistle ended," and the omission finds a parallel in the abandonment of the antiphons of the choir offices. The oblation of the elements, the ceremony of washing the hands, and the *secreta* are also gone. On the other hand there are a few new features—the Prayer for the King, and the connexion of the offertory anthem with the offering of the alms. But on the whole, the structure of this part of the Mass is well preserved. The case is somewhat different when we come to the Canon. This most venerable part of the service, in which no Pope or Church had ventured to change anything since the time of Gregory, was entirely rewritten by Cranmer and his colleagues. It is not easy to decide whether this was done for the sake of setting the English Church free from the domination of certain ideas which had long been associated with the Roman Canon, or because the English love of independence, to which the Reformation had given a new impulse, rebelled against the retention of a foreign rite in the most solemn act of our national worship. It is possible that as soon as the attempt was made to translate the Latin Canon, much of it was felt to be of uncertain value, and inferior, as a liturgical composition, to other parts of the ancient Order. The Canon which Cranmer substituted was on the whole formed upon the model of the Gregorian; it was one long prayer ending with the Lord's Prayer, and containing the three elements of intercession, commemoration, and oblation, which the Roman liturgy shared with all ancient liturgies whether Eastern or Western. But it abandoned the peculiarities and made good the imperfections of the Roman form; the intercessions for the living and the dead were no longer divided, the long list of names, chiefly of Roman saints and bishops, was omitted, and the Invocation of the Holy Spirit, lost or obscured in the Roman Canon, reappeared in its English successor. Lastly and chiefly, the narrative of the Institution, which in the Roman Canon had from an early time been strangely farsed and paraphrased, was now presented in the very words of the New Testament, and with special reference to the account which St. Paul declares himself to have received from the Lord. Yet in this as in other particulars the English Canon follows ecclesiastical if not Roman precedent; in the Mozarabic canon the Institution is commemorated in words very similar to those of the Book of Common Prayer, while the Greek liturgies approach more nearly to the English than to the Roman form [1].

After the long Prayer of Consecration the new English office found a place for the Order of Communion issued in 1548. A communion and a post-communion anthem are provided —the former invariable and consisting of the *Agnus Dei*, the latter a verse from the New Testament, to be selected out of twenty-two passages printed in full. Then comes a Thanksgiving, for which the Sarum and Roman rites made no provision, modelled upon Eastern forms; and instead of the venerable but now meaningless *Ite, missa est*, the new service ends with a solemn benediction [2].

Every one is familiar with the fate of this

---

[1] See Notes, p. 219 f.
[2] Some precedent for a final benediction is to be found in the York and Hereford Missals.

first English liturgy. In 1552 a second Prayer Book supplanted the Prayer Book of 1549, and while the Order for Mattins and Evensong suffered no material change, the Communion Service assumed quite another form, which on Elizabeth's accession became permanent, and still survives. The Introit, the Hosanna, the Intercession for the departed members of the Church, the Invocation of the Holy Spirit[1], the *Agnus Dei*, the post-communion anthem vanished; the ninefold *Kyrie* became tenfold, connecting itself with the Ten Commandments, which were now made to precede every celebration. But by far the most important changes were those of a structural character: the breaking up of the long canon, and the rearrangement of several of its component parts. Our present canon contains simply the commemoration of Redemption with the words of Institution. The Intercession for the Living was, in 1552, placed immediately after the Offertory; the Lord's Prayer and the Oblation follow the Communion of the People. A less remarkable displacement is the removal of the *Gloria in Excelsis* from the ante-communion to the post-communion, which may be explained by

[1] Notes, p. 220.

a desire to concentrate upon the end of the service the elements of praise and thanksgiving. From a liturgical point of view, these changes have brought about a very remarkable result, not perhaps contemplated by the revisers of 1552. The Communion Service of 1549 was as a whole a revised Sarum; it belonged to the Roman family of liturgies. This can scarcely be said of the present English liturgy; while it makes large use of Sarum and other ancient materials, in its structure it follows an order peculiar to itself. In other words, it heads a new liturgical family, and one which already has taken root, in slightly divergent forms, wherever the English tongue is spoken. There is no reason why English churchmen should regret the fact, or pine for a restoration of the Roman Mass. It was fitting that the Church of England should possess not merely an uniform use, but one which, while in accordance with ancient precedent in things essential, should proclaim her independence of foreign dictation in the order of her worship. It would have been a grave misfortune if the great English race had been tied for all time to customs and forms which rest ultimately upon the local traditions of an Italian Church.

While we are far from claiming either perfection or finality for the present English liturgy, we regard it with the loyal affection due to a national rite which has commended itself to the conscience of devout Englishmen for more than three centuries, and which is destined, as we believe, to surpass even the Roman Mass in the extent of its influence upon mankind.

CHAPTER IV.

THE MANUAL.

THE Manual was so named because it was a book which the parish priest needed to have in constant use. It contained the occasional offices, some of which he might be called upon to recite at any moment of the day or the night. Thus it answered to St. Augustine's definition of an *Enchiridion* : it was "a book not for the shelf or the cupboard, but for the hands[1]." The name, in its liturgical reference, was almost exclusively of English growth. On the continent the volume was usually known as the Pastoral (*pastorale, liber pastoralis*), the Sacramental (*sacramentale*, or sometimes, notwithstanding the ambiguity, *sacramentarium*), the *Agenda*, but more especially as the *Rituale*, the name by which it is still distinguished in the Roman Church. In England it seems to have always borne the title of *liber manualis* or *manuale*.

---

[1] *Ench.* 1. The word *Enchiridion* was used however as the designation of another liturgical book—the *Horae*, or Prymer. See Maskell, *Mon. Rit.* i. p. clxiii.

The Sarum Manual contained the services which in the English Prayer Book have been placed between the Order of Holy Communion and the Psalter, viz. the offices for administering Baptism and Confirmation, for the Solemnization of Matrimony, for the care of the sick, the dying, and the dead, and for the Churching of Women. To these were usually added various benedictions and other forms which the priest might need from time to time in the course of his daily ministrations. The book was unlike the Missal and the Breviary in that there was no one central service or group of services to which its other contents were subservient. Each of the services it contained had a separate history and purpose, and it will be necessary to deal with each by itself, although the accident of a common character, that of being occasional and not regular services, has brought them together into a single collection.

1. First among the offices of the Manual are those which relate to the Sacrament of Baptism and its supplementary rite, Confirmation.

The history of Baptism might easily fill a large volume, but for our present purpose the briefest outline may suffice. In the first age the circumstances which attended the initiation of converts were such as to exclude the use of ceremonial and even of devotional forms. It was performed by the side of some spring or river (Acts viii. 38), or in a bath (λουτρόν, Titus iii. 5) within doors (Acts xvi. 33), usually by immersion, but, where there was no sufficient supply of water, by the pouring of water on the head[1]. The candidate was received at his own desire, sometimes without preparation[2]. It has been doubted whether the words prescribed in Matt. xxviii. 19 were used in the first generations, since in the Acts believers are said to have been baptized in the Name of Jesus Christ, or of the Lord Jesus[3]; but on the other hand it may be urged that these terms involve the fuller form. Reference is made in the New Testament to the laying on of hands as a rite subsidiary to the act of Baptism[4], and possibly to the use of unction[5].

In the *Didache*, whilst neither the laying

---

[1] *Didache*, c. 7; see below.
[2] Acts viii. 36. The profession which precedes the baptism of the eunuch in the A. V. (v. 36) is an early interpolation.
[3] Acts ii. 38; viii. 16, &c.
[4] Acts viii. 17; xix. 6; Heb. vi. 2.
[5] 2 Cor. i. 21; 1 John ii. 20.

on of hands nor the anointing of the baptized is mentioned, we have the beginnings of an order for the ministration of the baptismal rite[1]. " As to Baptism, baptize on this wise. After ye have recited all this (i.e. the moral instruction of the previous chapters), baptize into the Name of the Father, the Son, and the Holy Ghost, in running water; but if thou hast not running water, baptize in other water, and if thou canst not do it in cold water, do it in hot; but if thou hast neither [in sufficient quantity], pour water on the head thrice in the Name of Father, Son, and Holy Ghost; and before the baptism let the baptizer fast and the baptizand, and some others if they can; the baptizand is to be desired to fast one or two days before." The directions are to some extent of a trivial character, a circumstance which may indicate a Jewish-Christian origin; but the preparation of the candidate by instruction and fasting is a step in advance towards later discipline.

Justin's account of the baptism of a convert in the middle of the second century carries us a little further. "We will describe," he writes[2], "the manner in which we dedicated ourselves to God. As many as are convinced

---

[1] C. 7 (Notes, p. 220).   [2] *Apol.* i. 61 (Notes, p. 220).

and believe our teaching to be true, and undertake to live according to it, are taught to beg of God with fasting and prayer the forgiveness of their past sins, whilst we pray and fast with them; then they are brought to a place where there is water and are regenerated after a manner of regeneration which we ourselves have undergone; for they make then their ablution in the water in the Name of the Sovereign God and Father of all, and of our Saviour Jesus Christ and the Holy Ghost. And this bath is called illumination ($\phi\omega\tau\iota\sigma\mu\delta s$)." Justin adds that the newly baptized are presently admitted to the Eucharist [1].

Another half-century brings us to Tertullian, from whose writings it is possible to collect a fairly complete description of the baptismal rites practised by the North African Church about the year 200. Baptism took place usually at Easter or during the fifty days after Easter, although any other day might be chosen in case of necessity [2]. After fasting and prayer, the candidate made before the bishop a solemn renunciation of the devil, his pomps, and his angels (" sub antistitis manu contestamur nos renuntiare

[1] *Apol.* c. 65.   [2] Tert. *de Bapt.* 18, 19 (Notes, p. 220).

diabolo et pompae et angelis eius ") [1]. Then he professed his faith in the Father, Son, and Holy Ghost, and in the Holy Church, and was thereupon thrice immersed ("ter mergitamur"). Subsequently he was anointed with hallowed unction and received the imposition of hands in order to obtain the gift of the Holy Spirit; he was signed with the cross, he tasted a mixture of milk and honey, a symbol of the land of promise to which he had been called, and last of all he partook of the Holy Eucharist [2]. Tertullian mentions, though he is disposed to discourage, the practice of infant baptism, and in connexion with it he speaks of sponsors [3].

Cyprian confirms much of Tertullian's testimony, mentioning the interrogatory creed offered to the candidates, the post-baptismal use of unction, and the imposition of hands [4]. But he is free from the scruples which Tertullian entertained as to the baptism of infants, and incidentally we learn from him that affusion was allowed instead of immersion in the case of the sick [5]. Both Tertullian and Cyprian recognize the preparatory stage of

[1] Tert. *de Coron. Mil.* 3; *de Bapt.* 6. [2] *De Bapt.* 7, 8.
[3] *De Resurr. Carn.* 8. [4] *Epp.* 70, 68, 64.
[5] *Ep.* 69.

catechumenate, distinguishing the *audientes* or *auditores* who retire from the church at an early stage in the mysteries; and Tertullian regards as characteristic of heresy the attempt to abridge unduly the course of preparation [1]. In the ante-Nicene age two or even three years seem not to have been thought an excessive probation; toward the end of this period the approved were known as *competentes* (i.e. fellow-candidates, Aug. *Serm.* 216), and received fuller instruction [2].

Of this instruction we have an example in Cyril's *Catecheses*. The preparatory course at Jerusalem in the middle of the fourth century lasted during the forty days of Lent, the baptisms taking place on Easter Eve [3]. Of the ceremony itself Cyril gives us a detailed account. The candidates assembled in the vestibule of the baptistery. There, facing West, with outstretched hands each of them repeated the form of renunciation: "I renounce thee, Satan, and all thy works, and all thy pomps, and all thy service." Then, turning to the East, he said, "I believe in the Father, and in the Son, and in the Holy Ghost, and in one baptism

---

[1] Tert. *Praescr.* 41; Cypr. *Ep.* 13.
[2] Conc. Elvir. *Can.* 62.
[3] *C. M.* i. (Notes, p. 221).

of repentance." After this the candidates entered the baptistery, and divesting themselves of their clothing, were anointed with consecrated oil. This done, each was led to the font (κολυμβήθρα), again confessed his faith, and thrice descended into the water and rose from it again, thus symbolically dying and rising again with Christ. On emerging from the font, the newly baptized were anointed with fragrant unguents (μύρῳ ἐχρίσθητε) on the forehead and organs of sense; this chrism was held to represent the sanctification of the soul by the Holy Ghost. No mention is made of the imposition of hands.

The *Apostolical Constitutions* contain several descriptions of Baptism [1]. The passages are too long to quote, but they correspond on the whole with Cyril's account; we read of the pre-baptismal and post-baptismal anointings, the first with oil, the second with chrism; both are to be performed by the bishop, and the second is in some way connected with imposition of hands, or regarded as a substitute for it [2]. On the whole, it seems as if the imposition of hands as a separate cere-

---
[1] iii. 15–17; vii. 22, 39 f.
[2] iii. 16; cp. Cyril, *Cat.* xvi. 26; and see Prof. Mason, *Baptism and Confirmation*, p. 341.

mony had by this time died out in Syria, or perhaps it would be more correct to say that the ceremonies of chrism and laying on of hands had been practically merged into one. In Egypt on the other hand, as in the North African Church of Cyprian's time, the two ceremonies were separately observed. The Coptic *Constitutions*, while providing for both anointings [1], direct the bishop to lay his hand on the baptized, saying, "Lord God ... make them worthy to be filled with Thy Holy Spirit;" after which he pours the "oil of thanksgiving" (= the chrism) into his own hand, and puts his hand on the head of the neophyte with the words, "I anoint thee with the holy anointing oil, from God the Father Almighty, and from Jesus Christ, and from the Holy Spirit," sealing him finally on the forehead with the sign of the cross.

With regard to the preparatory stages of the catechumenate, important help is offered to us in the *Pilgrimage of Silvia*. She tells us how the candidates gave their names eight weeks before Easter, and how, after an examination into their characters conducted by the bishop, they were exorcised [2], and during

---

[1] Mason, p. 250 f.
[2] Gamurrini, *Peregr. Silviae*, p. 72.

the rest of Lent received a complete course of instruction in Scripture, from Genesis onwards, the bishop explaining to them both the literal and spiritual interpretation. Instruction in the faith follows; in the fifth week the Creed is delivered, and at the end of the seventh each of the candidates repeats it before the bishop (*reddit symbolum episcopo*). The deeper mysteries of the baptismal rite are reserved for the instructions which follow the baptism and are delivered, as in the time of Cyril, during the octave of Easter.

We may now turn to the baptismal offices which were the direct ancestors of our present rite. If the Canons of Hippolytus may be taken as a guide to the early practice of the Roman Church, it is possible to form a fairly clear conception of a baptism at Rome in ante-Nicene times[1]. The Friday before the administration of the Sacrament is spent by the candidates fasting; on the Saturday they appear before the bishop, who extends his hands over them, and prays that the evil spirit may quit their bodies; he then breathes upon their faces and signs them on the breast, forehead, ears, and mouth. The following night is spent in a vigil service;

---
[1] Achelis, p. 92 ff.

at cockcrowing all assemble at the font, men and women, and the infants with their sponsors. The bishop thereupon blesses the oils, the "oil of exorcism" and the "oil of anointing" or "thanksgiving." Each candidate then renounces Satan, and is anointed by a presbyter with the oil of exorcism. Before going down into the water each says, "I believe, and bow myself before Thee and Thy full majesty, O Father, Son, and Holy Spirit." Then he steps down into the water and another presbyter, placing his hand on the candidates, asks, "Dost thou believe in God the Father Almighty? Dost thou believe in Jesus Christ the Son of God? &c. Dost thou believe in the Holy Ghost?" To each of these interrogatories the candidate answers "I believe," and after each answer he is dipped in the water, the presbyter who baptizes him repeating the baptismal words. As he rises the third time from the water he is signed with the chrism on his forehead, mouth, and breast, the presbyter saying, "I anoint thee in the name of the Father, and of the Son, and of the Holy Ghost." After this he resumes his garments, and enters the church, where he receives from the bishop the imposition of hands accompanied by the prayer that those on whom the gift of the remission of sins has already been bestowed may partake of the earnest of the kingdom of God. Finally, the neophytes receive the kiss of peace; then the Mass begins, and in due course they are communicated, receiving after their first Communion a taste of milk and honey as symbols of their new life in the family of God and of their future inheritance in the kingdom of heaven.

We are on more secure ground, and at the same time we find ourselves breathing an atmosphere which is nearer to that of our own mediaeval offices, when we turn to the Roman *Ordines*[1], and to the Sacramentaries of the seventh and eighth centuries. From these sources we may with some confidence frame an account of the baptismal ceremonies of the Roman Church at that date, as they were celebrated in connexion with Easter and Whitsuntide.

First came a solemn admission to the catechumenate. The ceremonies consisted of insufflation on the face, signing the forehead with the cross, imposition of the priest's hand upon the head with prayer, placing on the tongue a particle of salt which had been

[1] *Ord.* vii.

previously exorcised[1]. The catechumen thus admitted was called to undergo a series of examinations and instructions corresponding more or less fully to the Eastern *catecheses*, but at Rome known as *scrutinia*. These "scrutinies" began in the third week of Lent, and the Gelasian Sacramentary contains an interesting form of notice (*denuntiatio*) for the previous Sunday[2]: "Take notice, dearly beloved brethren, that the day of scrutiny on which our candidates for baptism (*electi*) are to begin their course of sacred instruction, is now at hand. Be so good as to assemble on such a day at noon, that (God helping us) we may be enabled to perform without reproach the heavenly mystery by which the devil is abolished with all his pomps, and the gate of kingdom of heaven is thrown open." A special Mass with intercessions for the candidates was provided for the Sunday before the first scrutiny[3]. When the day arrived and the candidates appeared at the church, their names were taken down; the males were placed on the right, the females on the left; after the collect at Mass they were exorcised, signed with the cross, and

---

[1] See the forms in Wilson, p. 46 ff.   [2] *Ib.* p. 45.
[3] *Ib.* p. 34.

received imposition of hands. Similar ceremonies marked each of the scrutinies except the third and the last. On the third a new feature was introduced. The day was known as *dies in apertione aurium,* and upon it took place the initiation of the baptizands in a knowledge of the Gospels, the Creed, and the Lord's Prayer. The ceremony—for since the candidates were now almost exclusively infants, it was little more—must have been an impressive one. After the Gradual, four deacons advanced to the altar preceded by lights and incense, each carrying one of the Gospels, which he deposited on one of the corners of the holy table. Then a priest came forward and explained the word *Gospel* and the symbols of the four Evangelists. A verse from each of the Gospels was then read and interpreted. Next came the delivery of the Creed; in the Sacramentary it is the Creed commonly called " Nicene," and it is repeated by the acolyte, either in Greek or Latin, according to the language of the catechumens or their parents. The ceremony ended with the delivery and exposition of the Lord's Prayer.

The seventh and last scrutiny took place on the morning of Easter Eve *(sabbato sancto, mane*), about 9 a.m. The candidates were once more exorcised, but on this occasion by a presbyter, and not as at previous scrutinies by acolytes or exorcists; and the exorcism was followed by the priest touching the nostrils and ears of the elect with his finger, moist with saliva, while he said, " Ephphatha, that is, Be opened." Then their breasts and backs were anointed with oil, and the renunciation of Satan followed in this form :

> " Dost thou renounce Satan ?"   " I renounce."
> " And all his works ?"   " I renounce."
> " And all his pomps ?"   " I renounce."

After it came a confession of faith, consisting of a repetition of the Creed (*redditio symboli*) by the priest in the name of the children about to be baptized.

The baptism followed later in the day. The Easter baptism was celebrated by the Pope himself in the baptistery of the Lateran. The rite began with a processional litany. Arrived at the font, the Pope blessed the water with prayers of considerable length, accompanied by the sign of the cross, insufflation, and the pouring of chrism into the water crosswise. Once more the "elect" was interrogated as to his faith :

"Dost thou believe in God the Father Almighty?"

"Dost thou believe also in Jesus Christ, His only Son, our Lord, Who was born and suffered?"

"Dost thou believe also in the Holy Ghost, the holy Church, the remission of sins, the resurrection of the flesh?"

Each candidate, having answered to every question "I believe," was then plunged three times into the water, while the baptismal words were uttered. After the immersion, each received from the priest the sign of the cross made with chrism on the crown of the head, and accompanied by the form, "Almighty God . . . Who hath regenerated thee with water and the Holy Ghost and hath given thee forgiveness of all thy sins, Himself anoint thee with the chrism of salvation, in Jesus Christ our Lord, unto eternal life." The neophytes were then brought to the bishop for confirmation. Laying his hand on them, the Pope offered the prayer for the sevenfold Spirit (*Spiritus septiformis*), which is familiar to us from its use in our present office; and this done, he signed each on the forehead with chrism, saying, "The sign of Christ unto eternal life." The Confirmation over, the procession was formed again, and entered the basilica; the first Mass of Easter began, the newly baptized received the Communion, and after it a mixture of milk and honey, which had been solemnly blessed. Throughout the octave of Easter they retained their white baptismal robes, and daily assisted in the Mass and at vespers; the whole week was regarded as a sacred fest'val.

We may now turn to the Sarum Use. In England during the middle ages the administration of baptism was practically limited to infants. Even in Anglo-Saxon times every infant was brought to the font within thirty or thirty-seven days after birth, under a heavy penalty[1]. The solemn celebration of the Sacrament on the eves of Easter and Pentecost continued, and children who were born not more than eight days before the festivals were reserved for those occasions; but at all other times baptism followed birth with the shortest possible interval[2]. For the same reason much of the ceremonial connected with the preparation of the catechumen, which was still preserved in the Roman rite of the seventh and eighth centuries, had disappeared in England before the Conquest; the scrutinies, the delivery and exposition of the Creed, find no place in

---

[1] Maskell, *Mon. Rit.* i. p. ccv.   [2] *Ib.* p. 29 f.

the Sarum books. On the other hand the great features of the rite remain intact. The Sarum office is fourfold; it begins with the form for making a catechumen (*ordo ad faciendum catechumenum*); there is a solemn benediction of the water (*benedictio fontis*), the baptism itself (*ritus baptizandi*) follows, and lastly the confirmation (*confirmatio puerorum*), which, though an episcopal function, was for the convenience of the parish priests inserted in the Manual, among the benedictions at the end of the book [1]. Theoretically these four offices formed, as they had always formed, a connected whole, but in practice they might be separately performed. Thus, in the case of the Easter and Pentecost baptisms, the Sarum rubric prescribed that the catechumenate should be given during the preceding week. The blessing of the water, which formed part of the Paschal and Pentecostal rite, was used as often as occasion required. The confirmation could follow the baptism immediately only if a bishop were present. Bede tells us how St. Cuthbert went round his diocese for the purpose of laying hands on the newly baptized [2], and this custom was maintained by the mediaeval

[1] Maskell, p. 34 *n*.   [2] *Vit. Cuthb.* 29.

episcopate, whilst parents were warned to bring their children to the bishop at the first opportunity, and at the latest within seven years after birth, under pain of suspension from Christian privileges [1].

The Sarum *Order for Making a Catechumen* directs the priest to meet the child at the church door where the office is performed. If it be a male, it is set on his right hand, if a female, on the left—a relic of the Roman mode of arranging catechumens at the scrutinies. Then the priest signs the child on the forehead and breast, and lays his hand on its head and prays. A grain of exorcised salt is placed in the infant's mouth; the child itself is exorcised in the words of the Roman Sacramentaries; prayers are added appropriate to the sex of the child. The Gospel of the blessing of little children is read from St. Matthew; the "Ephphatha" follows. Then the priest, sponsors (*compatres, commatres*), and bystanders repeat the *Pater, Ave*, and *Credo* (a reminiscence, possibly, of the *traditio* and *redditio symboli*); and the priest takes the child's right hand, and brings him into the church with the words, "Enter into the temple of God, that thou mayest

---

[1] Maskell, p. ccxiii f.

have life eternal, and live for ever and ever. Amen."

The *Benediction of the Font* begins with a litany, a survival of the processional litany of Easter Eve; after which the priest, being at the font, proceeds *more praefationis*, i. e. after the manner of the Preface in the Mass —a Gallican form which occurs in this place also in the "Gregorian" Sacramentary; in the course of this preface he uses the various ceremonies already described in our account of the Roman rite: crossing the water, breathing upon it, dropping wax into it from the lighted taper, and finally pouring into it holy oil and chrism, all in the form of the cross.

The infant is now brought to the font and the administration of the sacrament begins. The priest asks his name, and the threefold renunciation of Satan, his works, and his pomps is made. He is then anointed with holy oil on his breast and between the shoulders. The interrogative Creed is repeated in a somewhat longer form than that already quoted from the Gelasian Sacramentary[1]. To this the sponsors answer with a threefold *Credo*. The priest then

[1] For the form, see the writer's *Apostles' Creed*, p. 102 f.

asks, "What seekest thou?" Answer: "Baptism." "Wilt thou be baptized?" Answer: "I will." The name is once more demanded, and the priest, naming the child, plunges him thrice into the font, the first time at the word "Father," with the infant's face towards the North and his head to the East; the second time, at the word "Son," with the face to the South, the third time at the words "Holy Spirit," with the face towards the water. The godfathers take the child from the priest's hands, and the priest anoints him with chrism crosswise on the crown of the head, and puts upon him the chrisom (*vestis chrismalis*), with the words, "Receive a white robe, holy and without spot, and see thou bring it safe before the judgement-seat of our Lord Jesus Christ, that thou mayest have eternal life," &c. Lastly, a lighted taper is placed in the infant's hands, the priest saying, "Receive a lighted torch without reproach; guard thy baptism, keep the commandments, that when the Lord shall come to the marriage, thou mayest be able to meet Him with the saints in the heavenly courts, that thou mayest have eternal life," &c.

The Confirmation, which follows immediately (*statim, incontinenter*) if the bishop is present, is a remarkably short and simple office. It begins with the Psalm " Our help is in the Name of the Lord," after which, following the order of the Roman office, the bishop offers the prayer for the " septiform " Spirit, and then, having asked the baptismal name, he signs the child on the forehead with chrism, saying, "*N.*, I sign thee with the sign of the cross, and confirm thee with the chrism of salvation, In the Name," &c. A collect follows and after it the Psalm, "Lo, thus shall the man be blessed that feareth the Lord."

Such were the baptismal rites of the English Church before the Manual was superseded by the Book of Common Prayer. The first English Order for the Administration of Public Baptism undoubtedly contains a large proportion of new matter. It has been calculated that " hardly more than one-fourth part of the new office can be referred to the baptismal service of the ancient rituals [1]." But it is fair to explain that the new matter is largely homiletic, whereas the fourth, which is due to ancient sources, forms the backbone of the service. The changes were briefly the following: (1) The offices

[1] Gasquet and Bishop, p. 224.

for making a catechumen and for the administration of baptism were thrown into one. (2) Certain ancient ceremonies were abandoned, e. g. the administration of exorcised salt, the "*Ephphatha*," the infusion of foreign matter such as wax, oil, and chrism, into the water of the font, and the use of chrism in Confirmation. (3) Exhortations were introduced, explanatory of the Sacrament of Baptism and of the purpose of the several parts of the office, a feature not unknown to the baptismal rite of the ancient Gallican Church. On the other hand, the new office retained the most important features of the Sarum and Roman orders—the reception of the child at the church door and his solemn introduction into the church, the crossing before baptism, the exorcism, the threefold renunciation, the threefold confession of faith, the threefold immersion, the "white vesture commonly called the chrisom," the anointing of the newly baptized upon the crown of the head. In the benediction of the water, which, it was now ordered, should be changed once a month at the least, Sarum and Roman precedent was set aside, but the new forms were evidently based in great part on the Mozarabic rite, which supplied a finer and purer model[1]. The Confirmation service of 1549 follows closely in the steps of Sarum, excepting that the cross is no longer made with chrism, and the bishop is directed to lay his hand on the heads of the candidates as well as to sign them with the cross. The rubrics prefixed to the new office involve the postponement of Confirmation to a later age than that contemplated in the pre-Reformation order; no child is henceforth to be confirmed till he can give an account to the bishop or his deputy of the faith and duty of a Christian. This change, however, is one of policy, and not of form; in the latter the book of 1549 made no material alteration.

The baptismal offices of our present Prayer Book, which are based upon the revision of 1552, depart further from ancient precedents. Every one of the non-Scriptural ceremonies, which from the second century onwards had been growing up around the central act of baptism, has disappeared, except the signing with the cross, which the Church of England has stoutly maintained on the ground that it is not only a primitive but a singularly edifying practice[2]. On the other hand, the

[1] See Notes, p. 221 f.
[2] See note at the foot of the Ministration of Public Baptism to Infants.

ancient prayers and other forms retained in 1549 are with us still, and in regard to Confirmation the Church of England has gained immeasurably by a return to the Apostolic laying on of hands, and by a discipline which renders it possible to restore, in the case of persons baptized in infancy, the instruction and spiritual training formerly secured by the catechumenate.

2. After the offices for the baptism of children there followed in the Sarum Manual a short office for the Purification of Women (*Ordo ad purificandam mulierem post partum*). The law of Lev. xii. prescribes certain ceremonies of purification to which even the Mother of the Lord was careful to conform[1]. It was natural that the Church should perpetuate a custom sanctioned by so high an example; and there are indications from the fourth century at least of a belief that mothers ought to abstain from attendance at church until forty days after childbirth, and then to be solemnly readmitted. Indeed, according to the Canons of Hippolytus, a similar discipline existed in yet earlier times. Mothers are there directed not to present themselves for Communion till they have

[1] Luke ii. 22–24.

been purified. The purification is to take place on the twentieth or fortieth day according to the sex of the child, and during the interval the mother, if she desires to attend the House of God, must sit with the catechumens, and not among the faithful[1]. But if this harsh rule reflects the practice of the Church of Rome in early times, it would seem to have been practically obsolete before the date of the Roman mission to Kent. The point was one of those which perplexed Augustine of Canterbury, and his inquiry drew from Gregory the large-hearted answer, "If the mother entered the church to return thanks within an hour after her delivery she would not have sinned[2]." It will be observed that Gregory speaks of thanksgiving, and not of purification. The latter idea, however, was prominent in the mediaeval offices. According to the Sarum rite, the priest meets the woman at the church door, where the office is said; when it is over, she is brought within the church with the very words used at the introduction of a catechumen, "Enter into the temple of God." In the office of 1549 the tone is different,

---

[1] Achelis, p. 88.
[2] Bede, *H. E.* i. 27. See, however, p. 10 (supra).

the woman enters the church at once and comes "nigh unto the quire door": the Sarum Psalm and suffrages are retained, but the priest's address converts the service into an act of thanksgiving. In 1552, as the logical result of this change of purpose, a new title was substituted; the "Order of the Purification of Women" became "The Thanksgiving of Women after Child-birth, commonly called, The Churching of Women." It was perhaps intended that the common designation should gradually pass into disuse. But the word "churching" lends itself equally to either view of the office, and the use of the reformed Prayer Book for more than three centuries has set it free from its mediaeval associations. The English mother, when she is "churched," re-enters the House of God after a period of enforced absence, not in order to receive purification, but in the words of Gregory, the founder of the English Church, "to return thanks."

3. The act of Marriage does not absolutely demand the intervention of the Church. The essential ceremony is the contract by which the two parties openly accept one another as partners for life. Yet since the principles of the Gospel require the

faithful to connect every act or state of life with their higher life in GOD, it was impossible that so important an event should be left without the Church's sanction or the hallowing influence of a sacred rite. "It is fitting," writes Ignatius, Bishop of Antioch, in the early years of the second century, "that the bridegroom and the bride seek the consent of the bishop to their union, so that their marriage may be according to the Lord[1]." The approval of the bishop was naturally accompanied by his blessing. "How shall we describe," asks Tertullian, "the happiness of a marriage which is cemented by the Church, ratified by the oblation, and sealed with the benediction[2]?" Clement of Alexandria incidentally mentions that the nuptial blessing was conferred by the imposition of the priest's hand[3]. Ambrose of Milan, arguing against mixed marriages, asks, "Since matrimony must be hallowed by the priest's act of veiling the bride (*velamine sacerdotali*) and a benediction, how can we speak of it as existing when there is no agreement in the faith[4]?" One of the "African" canons rules that the bridegroom

[1] *Ad Polyc.* 5.
[3] *Paed.* iii. 11.
[2] *Ad Uxor.* ii. 8.
[4] *Ep.* 19.

and the bride shall be presented by their parents or friends (*paranymphi*), when they come to be blessed by the priest. Other ceremonies besides the veiling of the bride gradually attached themselves to the betrothal or the marriage. Most of these were inherited from Jewish or pagan custom. Tertullian refers to Rebekah (Gen. xxiv. 65) as exemplifying the use of the veil by betrothed women[1]; but the veiling of the bride with the *flammeum* was one of the ordinary ceremonies of a Roman marriage. So also was the practice which the Church subsequently adopted of crowning the bridegroom and bride with chaplets of leaves and flowers. The espousal of Rebekah was sealed by costly gifts[2]; Tobias and Sarah were wedded by the father of the bride taking her by the hand and giving her away[3]. The giving of a wedding ring (*annulus pronubus*) was a Roman and pagan ceremony, yet at Alexandria, as early as the time of Clement, a gold ring appears to have been the distinguishing mark of the Christian married woman[4].

Our first detailed account of a Christian

---

[1] *De Virg. vel.* 11: cf. Duchesne, *Origines*, p. 417, and for the present Eastern form, see *Euchologion*, p 241 f.
[2] Gen. xxiv. 47.   [3] Tobit vii. 12.   [4] *Paed.* iii. 11.

marriage comes from a Roman bishop of the ninth century (Nicolas I, A. D. 866)[1]. He speaks of (1) the espousals (*sponsalia*) followed by the giving of the ring, and of a marriage deed which secured a dowry to the bride; (2) the nuptials (*nuptialia foedera*), transacted in the church, and marked by oblations presented to God through the priest, the benediction of the espoused, the veiling of the bride, and the crowning of both. The nuptials properly so called, i. e. the sequel to the espousals, were connected with the celebration of the Eucharist, and provision for a nuptial Mass is made in the Leonian and Gelasian Sacramentaries; in the former it is described as the *velatio*, in the latter as the *actio, nuptialis*[2]. The collect, *secreta*, and other special devotions are appropriate to the occasion; the nuptial benediction follows the Lord's Prayer of the Canon, coming between the consecration and the communion of the newly married pair; in the Gelasian Mass a second and shorter benediction follows the Communion. The Sacramentaries contain no ceremonial directions, nor do they supply a form of

[1] *Resp. ad Cons. Bulg.* 3; cp. Duchesne, *Origines*, p. 414 f.
[2] Muratori, *Liturg. Rom. Vet.* i. pp. 446, 721.

espousals. For these we must go to the mediaeval English books. In the Sarum Missal we find the *ordo sponsalium*, succeeded by the nuptial Mass, the latter being in the main the Mass of the Holy Trinity, with materials worked into it from the old *velatio nuptialis* of the Roman Sacramentaries; an office substantially the same is to be found in the Sarum Manual. We will follow the order of the Manual [1].

The espousals begin by the priest meeting the bridal party at the door of the church and "bidding the banns" in the English tongue ("banna dicens in lingua materna"). To "bid banns" is simply to give public notice, and the banns of the Sarum espousals consist of the address which opens with the familiar words, "Dearly beloved, we are gathered together here ... to join together this man and this woman in holy matrimony." The banns are repeated in this form on three not consecutive holy days, during Mass. If no objection is alleged, the priest proceeds, still using the mother tongue, "Wilt thou have this woman ... wilt thou have this man?" and the man and woman are then taught [2] to

---

[1] Maskell, *Mon. Rit.* i. p. 42 ff.
[2] See Notes, p. 222.

pledge one another in English words almost identical with the quaint formulae of our present Marriage Service. Then the man places gold and silver with the ring on the priest's book, and if the ring has not been blessed already, it receives a benediction and is sprinkled with holy water. The ring is then placed by the man as our present rubric directs, except that he puts it on the first finger as he names the Father, and so on, pronouncing the "Amen" when he reaches the fourth. Almost the only novelty in the Espousals of 1549 is the joining of the right hands of the espoused by the priest, together with the sentence of marriage which follows.

So far the Sarum service was said at the church door; after the blessing of the espousals, the party entered the church and proceeded to the altar step, the priest and his ministers saying as they went the Psalm *Beati omnes*. In the prayers which succeed, the Prayer Book generally follows Sarum guidance, until we come to the nuptial Mass. The new book provided no special *missa*; our Reformers were content with ordering that "the new-married persons (the same day of their marriage) must receive the holy communion," and for this direction our present book substitutes a simple recommendation to receive it "at the time of their marriage, or at the first opportunity after their marriage." In the Sarum rite, immediately after the prayers at the altar step, the bridegroom and the bride enter the presbytery, taking their places on the south side between the choir and the altar, and Mass begins with the introit. The formal benediction of the marriage is given, as in the old Sacramentaries, between consecration and communion. The *pax* is offered by the priest to the bridegroom and by him to the bride. After Mass, they partake together of bread and wine which have been blessed, and so depart, the priest afterwards visiting their house and blessing them there.

None of our occasional services departs so little from the Sarum form as the Solemnization of Matrimony, and none underwent so little change between 1549 and 1662, when the Prayer Book reached its present state. Excepting the loss of the nuptial Mass, Englishmen are married in these last years of the nineteenth century nearly as they were married at the beginning of the thirteenth; even the quaint English of the espousals has been suffered to remain without any considerable change. The fact is important, inasmuch as it reveals the conservative policy which on the whole guided our Reformers. In the marriage service of the mediaeval Church there was little which savoured of superstition or error in belief, and therefore little was changed. In this respect it stands in strong contrast to the offices which we are about to consider, in which there were few devotions that could be safely preserved in their mediaeval form.

4. The Manual of the Church of Salisbury contains offices for the visitation, unction, and communion of the sick, for the commendation of the soul in the article of death and after departure, and for the burial of the dead.

From the first the visitation of the sick was a recognized duty of the officers of the Church. The words "I was sick, and ye visited Me," together with the example of the Lord's unfailing compassion for all varieties of human suffering, left an impression which could not easily be effaced. In the Apostolic age the Church possessed gifts of healing which enabled her to follow in the Master's steps. "They shall lay their hands on the sick, and they shall recover," is one of the last promises attributed to the ascending Christ[1]. Another mode of exercising the gift was by the use of oil. "Is any sick?" (writes St. James[2]) "let him call for the presbyters of the Church, and let them pray over him, anointing him with oil in the name of the Lord, and the prayer of faith shall restore the sufferer" (σώσει τὸν κάμνοντα). The use of oil had been connected with the healing of the sick in the early ministry of the Apostles[3], and continued to be occasionally employed both by the Church and some heretical sects. Certain Gnostics of the second century anointed the dying with oil and water, adding magical formulas[4]. A more legitimate use of the symbol was made by Catholic Christians in cases where recovery was still possible. Tertullian claims that the Emperor Septimius Severus was restored to health through the prayers of a Christian who anointed him with oil in the name of Christ[5]. Toward the end of the fourth century oil taken from the church lamps was regarded as a specific; at the beginning of the sixth, Caesarius, Bishop of Arles, in time of common sickness, recommends the head of a family to anoint his

[1] Mark xvi. 18.   [2] v. 14, 15.   [3] Mark vi. 13.
[4] Iren. i. 21. 5.   [5] *Ad Scap.* 4.

household with oil which had been blessed. But there is no evidence of any continuous tradition on the lines of St. James's direction, partly perhaps because the practice was originally confined to communities of Christian Jews, partly on account of the comparatively limited circulation of the Epistle in early times. On the other hand there is evidence that the sick were not neglected by the clergy; their wants, both material and spiritual, received attention from the first. Polycarp, for example, charges the presbyters of Philippi [1] "that they visit all the sick." The contemporary biographer of St. Augustine mentions that the great Bishop of Hippo was always ready to lay his hands on the sick and pray for them, and when summoned to this duty went without delay [2].

In the Roman Sacramentaries we meet at length with forms of prayer for use both in the sick man's house (*orationes super infirmum in domo*), and in church at a special Mass offered in his behalf (*orationes ad missam pro infirmo*), together with a prayer for convalescents (*oratio pro reddita sanitate*) [3]. The Gelasian Sacramentary [4] bears witness also to

[1] C. 6. [2] *Vit.* c. 33.
[3] See the Gelasian forms in Wilson, p. 281 f.
[4] *Ib.* p. 70.

the use of oil for the restoration of the sick from spiritual as well as bodily maladies (*ad evacuandos omnes dolores, omnem infirmitatem, omnem aegritudinem mentis et corporis*); but though the form occurs amongst the benedictions of the various oils which were blessed annually on the Thursday before Easter, there is no corresponding office for the administration. Muratori is guilty of something like an anachronism when he refers in his index to this oil as prepared for "Extreme Unction"; in the Sacramentary it is described simply as "oil for anointing the sick" (*istud oleum ad unguendos infirmos*) [1].

In the Sarum Manual the parish priest is supplied with complete offices both for Visitation and for Unction [2]. When called to visit the sick the priest went with his ministers to the house, saying on the way the seven penitential Psalms with the antiphon, "Remember not, Lord, our offences." Reaching the house he invoked peace upon it, and on entering the sick man's presence, sprinkled him with holy water, saying the *Kyrie*, Lord's Prayer, and suffrages, as they are found in our present form of Visitation, and a number

---

[1] See however the *Excerpt. Egbert.* § 21, which prescribe the administration by a priest.
[2] Maskell, *Mon. Rit.* i. p. 66 ff.

of collects, among which we recognize several of the Gelasian prayers for the sick. The priest proceeded to examine the sick person as to his faith, using either a summary of the *Quicunque*, or, in the case of the illiterate, a simpler form based on the Apostles' Creed; he then exhorted him to charity and patience, heard his confession and gave him absolution, concluding with prayers and a blessing.

The Unction of the Sick followed. The office begins with a Psalm accompanied by the antiphon, "O Saviour of the world." In anointing, the priest, dipping the thumb of his right hand into the oil, applied it to the organs of the senses, the feet, and the loins, and at each application offered the prayer "By this unction, of His own most tender mercy, may the Lord forgive thee whatever sins thou hast committed by the sense of sight" [hearing, taste, &c., as the case might be]. Lastly, the priest prayed for the restoration of the sick to spiritual and bodily health. After unction the Sacrament of the Body of Christ was exhibited to the sufferer, and he was asked whether he believed the true Body and Blood of Christ to be present under the form of bread; upon his assent, he was communicated, unless circumstances prevented him from receiving, when the priest was bidden to say, "Brother, in this case it suffices for thee to have a true faith and good will; believe only, and thou hast eaten[1]."

Dr. Rock[2] draws a goodly picture of the mediaeval rector or vicar proceeding to the house of the sick, sometimes with a procession of surpliced clerks, with uplifted cross, tinkling hand-bell, and lighted tapers, while the country folk kneel as he passes, and join their prayers with the Gregorian tones which accompany the penitential Psalms; whilst at other times, when called to some poor cottage among the hills or accessible only by rugged roads, the village priest would mount his horse, with the pyx in a silk bag slung round his neck, and a single lighted taper in a lantern with a bell attached to it, suspended from the neck of his horse. Still more attractive is the jealous care of the mediaeval Church that her sick members should not die without the last sacraments or receive them without instruction and preparation. English synods forbade the parish priest to pass a single night away from his parish without reasonable cause, or without a deputy[3]; whilst

[1] The words are founded on St. Augustine's dictum, *Tract. in S. Joann.* xxv. 12.
[2] *Church of our Fathers*, ii. p. 462 f.
[3] Maskell, *Mon. Rit.* i. p. ccxxxvii.

for his assistance in the instruction of the sick, he was furnished with English exhortations, remarkable for their simplicity, tenderness, and evangelical tone [1].

For the last extremity the Manual provides another office, the "Commendation of a Soul in the Article of Death." It begins with a litany, specially adapted for the case of the dying; after which follows the *Proficiscere anima Christiana*, and short suffrages for the release of the departing spirit.

Thus far the reformed ritual follows in the track of the Sarum offices. The new Visitation of the Sick is distinctly on the lines of the old; the Unction of the Sick was retained in 1549 although in a simpler and discretionary form, the priest being directed to anoint the sick person upon the forehead or breast only, and to give unction only where it was desired by the sufferer himself. No provision, however, was made for the benediction of the oil; "even extreme unction," the Romanists complained in 1551, "is administered with unconsecrated oil [2]." The Communion of the Sick was also retained, but the fear of an illegitimate use of the reserved Sacrament

---

[1] Maskell, iii. p. 353 ff. (Notes, p. 222 f.).
[2] Gasquet and Bishop, p. 273.

led our Reformers in 1549 to restrict reservation to the day on which the elements were consecrated, and three years afterwards to abandon it altogether, substituting a celebration in the sick man's room. Some of the extreme men on the anti-Roman side were prepared to go further: "let the sick," writes Coverdale, "satisfy himself with the general breaking of bread whereof he was a partaker with the whole congregation"; but the majority preferred under the circumstances to sanction private celebrations, rarely as they had been used by the ancient Church, rather than to withhold the *Viaticum* from the dying. To the sick the new order was on the whole a gain; they retained the blessing of a sacramental communion in their houses, and they acquired the new privilege of assisting in the celebration so far as their strength permitted.

From offices for the sick and dying we pass by a natural step to the Order for the Burial of the Dead. Here the mediaeval Church surpassed herself in the wealth of her devotions; but unhappily her services did not lend themselves to the older and truer view of death which the English reformers were determined to revive.

Nothing more sharply distinguished the

early Christians from their pagan neighbours than the attitude of the faithful toward their dead. St. Paul, in the earliest of his Epistles[1], warns his converts "not to be sorry" for the dead, "as the rest" of the world "who have no hope." For believers to die was to depart and be with Christ; it was to enter Paradise; death could not separate them from the love of God or from the fellowship of the saints; on the contrary it was the beginning of a fuller life, the moment when the goal was attained and the labours of the course were ended. The earlier treatment of the dead is deeply coloured by these essentially Christian views. The pagan cremated his dead; Christians preferred "the old and better custom of burying them[2]." The Church turned the gloom of the funeral into a triumph; when circumstances permitted, palms and flowers, lights and incense, psalms and anthems, attended the body to its resting-place. Between death and burial the religious exercises were expressive of peace and hope: the clergy offered prayer around the body[3], a last kiss of peace was given; the night which intervened between death and interment was brightened by psal-

---

[1] 1 Thess. iv. 13.   [2] Min. Fel. *Octav.* 65.
[3] Tert. *de Anim.* 51.

mody, and before the dead was committed to the tomb, the Eucharist was offered for him [1]. No early liturgy is without a commemoration of the departed. But these ancient prayers and offerings for the dead implied no doubt of the felicity of those who "depart hence in the Lord"; they were simply the expression of the strong belief that death sets up no real barrier between the faithful, and that the dead in Christ, not having yet reached "their perfect consummation and bliss," may still be commended to the mercy and love of God. It is unnecessary here to enter into any discussion of this belief; but we may note that it is not to be identified with that doctrine of the intermediate state which was dominant in the Western Church from the sixth century to the sixteenth. We can put our finger on the source of this later teaching. A hint dropped by St. Augustine that some of the faithful may possibly be called after death to pass through a purifying fire (*ignis purgatorius*) [2], was raised to the rank of a dogma by Gregory the Great, the founder of the English Church [3]. From the moment of its conversion, Anglo-Saxon Eng-

---

[1] Aug. *Confess.* ix. 12.   [2] *Enchir.* 69.
[3] *Dial.* iv. 39; *Moral.* ix. 34.

land was darkened by the gloom which this unhappy surmise cast over the state of the dead. Dr. Rock points with triumph [1] to her universal acceptance of purgatory; it would have been strange indeed if she had not accepted a doctrine which was brought to her shores by the men who gave her the Christian faith. The terrible visions of the unseen life described by Bede reveal the hold which the doctrine already had upon the popular imagination. One Dryhthelm[2], whose spirit had visited the unseen world and afterwards returned to life, used to tell how he had seen the souls of the departed in a region where they were scorched on the one hand by raging flames and frozen by intolerable cold upon the other. His guide had explained that this was the place of chastisement where those who had postponed confession and amendment to the end of life were disciplined, till at the day of judgement they were permitted to enter the kingdom of heaven. Many, however, it was added, were released before the great day, through the prayers, alms, and fasting of the living, and above all by the celebration of Masses. Under this belief the whole system

[1] *Church of our Fathers*, ii. 288.
[2] Bede, *H. E.* v. 12.

of devotions connected with death and burial took shape in the mediaeval Church, and it is not surprising that the atmosphere of peace and hope and triumph which had characterised the earlier treatment of the dead was exchanged for one of gloomy apprehension.

The Gelasian Sacramentary supplies the earliest extant forms for use with the dying and after death[1]. It contains commendations of the departing soul, prayers after death, before burial, and after burial, and a considerable number of special *missae*. These devotions breathe upon the whole the spirit of the earlier belief, although we notice in them, and still more in some of the Gregorian forms, occasional indications of the influence of the new teaching.

In the Sarum Manual the rites which follow death begin with a *Commendatio animarum*, distinct from the commendation of the soul in the article of death which has been already described, and consisting of Psalms intermingled with prayers for the departed. The body is then washed and spread upon a bier; vespers for the day are said, followed by the vigils of the dead, the special vespers and special mattins commonly known from their respective

[1] Wilson, p. 295 f.

antiphons as the *Placebo* and the *Dirige* or "dirge." It is then carried in procession to the church, accompanied by a cross-bearer and acolytes with lighted tapers, a man with a bell going before the corpse to invite the prayers of the passers-by; after him come the priest and his ministers, in albs, singing Psalms, the body being followed by friends of the deceased bearing torches, with the mourners in black cloaks. In the church the dead is laid with his feet towards the high altar. Mass is then said, or if it be too late for Mass, the body remains in the church until the first Mass of the following day. After Mass the priest puts off his chasuble, and the special office for the burial of the dead (*Inhumatio defuncti*) begins. The service falls into three divisions; the first to be said in church at the head of the body, the second on the way to the grave, the third at the grave itself. The first consists of antiphons, Kyries, and prayers, the precentor and choir assisting, while the priest censes the body and sprinkles it with holy water. On the way to the grave, the Psalms *In exitu Israel* and *Ad te, Domine, levavi* are sung, and the old suffrages said, " Eternal rest grant them, Lord, and let perpetual light shine upon them." The grave, of which the priest had previously cut the first sod in the form of a cross, is now opened with the psalm *Confitemini, Domino, quia bonus*, and the antiphon "Open to me the gates of righteousness." Then, the grave having been blessed and aspersed, prayers for the departed follow, and the priest pronounces a final absolution. Earth is thrown crosswise on the body, and the interment is completed during the singing of a psalm; after which the priest says, "I commend thy soul to God the Father Almighty; earth to earth, ashes to ashes, dust to dust: in the Name of the Father and of the Son and of the Holy Ghost." On returning to the church the clerks sing the penitential Psalms or the *De profundis*, and the priest dismisses them with the prayer, "May the soul of this person and the souls of all the faithful departed rest in peace."

The office is not wanting in beauty, and many of the prayers are ancient, only one or two referring to the purgatorial fire in repulsive terms[1]; but it dwells with a wearisome monotony on the terrors of death and the uncertainty of the state of the departed. Even the singing of the choir did not

[1] See e.g. Maskell, *Mon. Rit.* i. pp. 125, 128.

brighten the gloom; no one who has listened to the Gregorian music of a continental funeral will have forgotten the depressing effect. The friends left the grave with no "sure and certain hope"; on the contrary, there was the terrible possibility that notwithstanding the funeral Mass and the many prayers offered for the departed, he was still in suffering and must continue so for many a year. Moreover, the gloom of the funeral rites did not end with the burial of the dead; the vigils of the dead and Masses for his soul were said from time to time throughout the following month, specially on the third, seventh, and thirtieth day. "With these observances of what was called 'the month's mind,' ended the funeral obsequies from the earliest to the latest days of [Roman] Catholic England [1]."

The whole system was inseparably connected in the national mind with the doctrine of purgatory in its coarsest and most mischievous form, and the Reformers are scarcely to be blamed for having submitted the burial offices to a more drastic revision than any other group of ancient services. Indeed, the moderation of their first attempt at a reform

[1] Rock, ii. 517 f.

is worthy of all praise. In the Prayer Book of 1549 the Commendation of departed souls disappears, but prayers for the deceased are retained throughout the new Order for Burial, and sometimes in the very words of the ancient forms. The first Prayer Book also provided for "the Celebration of the Holy Communion, when there is a burial of the dead," and here again old materials were freely used. Nevertheless the change of tone was immense. The new office breathed the primitive spirit of peace and hope; with prayers for the departed brother it mingled thanksgivings for his happiness, and the great lesson from 1 Cor. xv. restored the Apostolic note of triumph over death as a conquered enemy.

In the second Prayer Book the work of reconstruction was carried much further; the special forms for use at a funeral Celebration were abandoned, and every vestige of direct intercession for the dead was swept away. The result has been to crush out of English life the mediaeval belief in a purgatorial fire, but at the cost of sacrificing practices undoubtedly dear to the early Church and of eliminating from English Christianity one important side of the ancient doctrine of the intermediate state. It has left us, however, an Order for the Burial of the Dead which, notwithstanding these defects, is more consolatory, more inspiring, and, upon the whole, nearer to the spirit of the primitive belief than any which was known in England from the days of Augustine of Canterbury to the middle of the sixteenth century [1].

[1] Canon Wordsworth reminds me that the consequences of the omission of a form for Celebration at burials "began at once to be felt and as far as possible supplied. At the funeral of Henry II, king of France, which was solemnized in St. Paul's, Parker, Barlow, Scory, the Lord Chamberlain, and certain noblemen received the Communion (Sept. 9, 1559). And not long afterwards (Dec. 5, 1559), the sisters of Lady Jane Grey among others received the Sacrament at their brother's funeral at Westminster, when Jewel was the preacher, and Dr. May, Dean of St. Paul's, the celebrant (Strype, *Annals*, 1. cc. 9, 15). Further, in the next year, (April 6, 1560), so far as the Queen's power could go, she authorized the use of such a service at the Universities, and at Winchester and Eton (Cardwell, *Doc. Ann.* no. 50; *Liturgical Services of Queen Elizabeth*, p. 430 f.). And the use has been allowed in cathedral and other churches, possibly by Overall (Nicholls, p. 65), and in more recent times certainly by Bishop Chr. Wordsworth of Lincoln (1872), Bishop Mackarness of Oxford (1882); and the present Bishop of Salisbury in Synod (1896) authorized his clergy to apply to him for permission as occasion arose."

CHAPTER V.

THE PROCESSIONAL.

THE Procession occupied an important place in the worship of the Church of England from the earliest time to the middle of the sixteenth century. Not only on special occasions, such as the burial of the dead, and the consecration of churches and churchyards, but on the great festivals of the Christian Year, and even on ordinary Sundays and certain *feriae*, processions were conducted with prescribed ceremonies and forms of psalmody and prayer[1]. Every Sunday before Mass there was a procession in the church. Starting from the choir, it usually passed down the south aisle to the font, returning up the nave to the rood, where the English bidding prayer was said. A similar order, with some variations in detail, and the omission of the bidding prayer, was observed

[1] *Processionale ad Usum Sarum*, ed. Henderson, pref. p. xi.

on certain holy days not Sundays. Processions also frequently occurred at vespers, e. g. on all Saturdays from Trinity to Advent. Wednesdays and Fridays in Lent, Holy Week and Easter, and the Rogation Days, were all marked in this way. On Palm Sunday, Ascension Day, and Corpus Christi the procession paraded the churchyard; on the Rogation Days and St. Mark's Day it went beyond the churchyard, into the streets and open country. The party consisted of boys in surplices carrying holy water, men in albs and amices, the officiating priest in a silk cope. But the vestments varied in richness and colour according to the occasion or season; on great feasts the whole choir were vested in silk copes. On certain days lighted tapers were carried, and incense was swung; banners accompanied the processions of Palm Sunday, Rogation Days, Ascension Day, and Corpus Christi; relics were occasionally borne along. On Ash Wednesday, Thursday in Holy Week, and the Rogation Days, a sermon might be added, if the priest thought good. Otherwise, with the exception of the concluding collect, the service was entirely musical, consisting of responds, antiphons, and proses, sometimes of psalms, hymns, or litanies. For each day in the year to which a procession was assigned the Processional supplied an order of service with full ritual directions.

Enough perhaps has been said to show how great a blow was struck at the existing system of popular worship when a royal injunction, in 1547, abolished liturgical processions of every kind. The young King, acting doubtless on Cranmer's suggestion, based his prohibition on certain abuses and disadvantages which had been found to attend their use; he was moved by a desire " to avoid all contention and strife which heretofore hath risen among the King's majesty's subjects in sundry places of his realms and dominions by reason of fond courtesy and challenging of places in procession, and also that they may the more quietly hear that which is said or sung to their edifying[1]." For this cause, the injunction proceeds, "they shall not from henceforth in any parish church at any time use any procession about the church or churchyard or other place, but immediately before High Mass the priests with other of the quire shall kneel in the midst of the church and sing or say plainly

[1] Cranmer's *Works* (Parker Soc.), ii. p. 502.

and distinctly the Litany, which is set forth in English, with the suffrages following."

The English Litany then is the sole direct representative in our present Prayer Book of the mediaeval Processional. "The Procession services," Mr. Bradshaw writes[1], "correspond to our hymns or anthems sung before the Litany which precedes the Communion Service in the morning and after the third Collect in the evening;" and this is of course the case in so far as the anthem or hymn occupies a place in our services which corresponds generally with that which was anciently given to the procession. But the anthem was not immediately substituted for the procession; indeed, no rubrical provision was made for it until the final revision of the Prayer Book in 1661. On the other hand, the singing of the Litany on Sundays between Mattins and Mass was, as we have seen, definitely ordered with the view of filling up the gap left by the abolition of the Sunday procession; and the Litany itself is based on forms which, though they are to be found also in the other Service-books, belong of right to the Processional.

The Litany (*letania, laetania*) derives its name from the Greek word λιτανεία, meaning

---

[1] Prothero, *Memoir*, p. 423.

"supplication." The word occurs in Hellenistic Greek in the sense of a supplication offered to GOD in time of need or peril, e. g. in 2 Macc. iii. 20 we read: "All, stretching forth their hands towards heaven, made their solemn supplication" (ἐποιοῦντο τὴν λιτανείαν). St. Basil speaks of the use of such litanies by the clergy of Neo-Caesarea [1], intimating that they were of comparatively recent introduction, later than the days of Gregory Thaumaturgus, who died about 270. The Eastern liturgies contain supplications somewhat analogous in form to those of the later Western litanies, but known as *Ectenae* (ἐκτεναί), *Synaptae* (συναπταί), or *Irenica* (εἰρηνικά), and such "missal litanies" are also to be found in Western liturgical uses which were framed more or less under Eastern influences; those, for example, of Milan and of Spain, where they appear under the names of *preces* or *preces pacificae*. The characteristic feature of these devotions is a refrain, usually the *Kyrie eleison*, following each of a series of petitions or invitations to intercession and prayer. In Greek liturgical *ectenae* the litany is generally of the nature of a bidding prayer, in which the deacon

[1] *Ep.* 207, § 4.

bids and the people respond; the Western *preces*, on the other hand, assume the form of direct supplication [1].

The word "litany," however, does not appear in connexion with Missal intercessions of either type. Its normal use is limited to Western processional supplications; so complete is the identification that *letania* and *processio* are often convertible terms. It is from the processional litany that the English litany may claim to be directly descended.

Two annual processions accompanied by litanies can be traced back to the fifth and sixth centuries, the former at first peculiar to the Gallican Churches, the latter to the Church of Rome. About the year 470 Vienne was disturbed by frequent earthquakes, the last throes of the volcanic movements in Auvergne. While the Viennese were agitated by these troubles, another supervened. On Easter Eve, during the vigil service, a fire broke out in the palace within the walls of the city; the people fled panic-stricken, leaving their bishop, Mamertus, alone before the altar. Mamertus, as he knelt there, vowed that he would organise "litanies" on the three days pre-

[1] Neale, *Essays*, pp. 73, 141 ff.

ceding the coming Feast of the Ascension. His vow was kept; in the words of Gregory of Tours[1], "he proclaimed a fast, appointed a form of prayer, arranged the order of the processions and supplications." The result seemed to justify the means, for the earthquakes ceased. From that time Ascensiontide rogations were observed annually at Vienne, and other Gallican dioceses followed the example. In England, probably through Gallican influence, they were known before the time of Bede, who died on the last of the "gang days," when, as Cuthbert explains, "they walked from terce onwards with the relics of the saints[2]." Indeed the observance would seem to have been of longer standing, for in 747, the Council of Clovesho, while pressing upon the English Church the observance of the Roman litany, adds, "Likewise, *after the custom of our forefathers*, let the three days before the Ascension of the Lord into heaven be kept by fasting till the ninth hour and by the celebration of the Mass... let them be marked by the sign of Christ's passion and the relics of the saints being carried publicly, while all the people on

---

[1] *Hist.* ii. 34.
[2] Mayor and Lumby, pp. 178, 406.

bended knees implore God's pardon for their sins[1]."

At Rome, the Ascensiontide Rogations were not introduced before the time of Charlemagne. Meanwhile, Rome had a yearly litany of her own, the origin of which is usually ascribed to Gregory. The day was April 25, the festival of St. Mark. In a sermon preached on St. Mark's Eve, 590, when the plague was raging at Rome, Gregory[2] announced the arrangements which had been made for a "septiform" procession on the following day. The clergy were to start from St. John the Baptist's Church, the men from St. Marcellinus, the monks from the Church of SS. John and Paul, the virgins from the Church of SS. Cosmas and Damian, the married women from St. Stephen's, the widows from St. Vitalis', the poor and the children from St. Caecilia's; and the seven processions were to meet in one great gathering at the Church of St. Mary Major. The selection of the day seems to have been determined by local circumstances: it had been marked in pagan times by the festival of the Robigalia, when the gods were

---

[1] Haddan and Stubbs, iii. p. 368.
[2] Greg. M. *Ep.* ii. 9.

supplicated to keep mildew from the crops; and in using the day for a procession the Roman Church followed her customary policy of grafting Christian institutions upon an older stock. Whether the idea was Gregory's or was merely developed and matured by him, the St. Mark's Day litany became a permanent observance at Rome, and with necessary changes it established itself in other Churches, at Milan, in Frankland, and in England. Interesting traces of the use of the St. Mark's Day procession are preserved in the St. Gallen MS. of the Gelasian Sacramentary[1], and in Sacramentaries of the Gregorian type, but only the collects to be offered at the "stations" find a place in these collections; the litanies themselves are wanting. In another of his letters Gregory[2] tells that the litany of St. Mark's Day was generally known as the "Greater." The name is important, because it implies that other litanies were in use at Rome in Gregory's time. We have already mentioned the litany which accompanied the procession to the font on Easter Eve. "Incipit clerus litania[m]," the Gelasian rubric

---

[1] Wilson, pp. xlv, 340; Muratori, i. pp. 11, 80. See also P. and W. i. p. dccclxxxvii f.; iii. p. 264.   [2] *Ep.* xi. 2.

THE PROCESSIONAL. 181

runs, " et procedit sacerdos de sacrario "—the clerks begin the litany, as the priest goes down from the vestry to the font. The Sarum Processional provides a litany for every Wednesday and Friday in Lent. A litany was also used at ordinations, before extreme unction and in funeral processions [1]. Finally, one was sung in procession at times of public necessity, in drought, in bad weather, in plague or war. It was such an occasion which called forth the first draft of the present English litany. In 1543 heavy rains at harvest-time ruined the crops, and a famine was thought to be imminent. A procession was ordered, but the order was not obeyed to the satisfaction of the King; in some places the Sarum litany was sung, in others they used the versions of the Latin litany which were found in the Primers. The incident suggested the need of an authorized English version of this popular devotion, and the next year an Order in Council committed to Cranmer the task of preparing such a form [2]. The result was the English litany of 1544; and it was this litany which with a few changes was embodied in the Prayer

[1] Sarum Processional, p. 166.
[2] Hook, *Lives of the Archbishops*, ser. ii. vol. ii. p. 203.

Book of 1549. Processions had meanwhile been suppressed, but the "General Supplication" written for processional use has happily survived, and is still appointed to be said or sung on Sundays, on the days of the *stationes*, and at other times at the discretion of the ordinary.

The germ of all processional litanies is the *Kyrie eleison*. The words, derived from the Greek Psalter (e.g. Ps. xl. (xli.) 4 Κύριε, ἐλέησον), passed in their Greek form into the West, and were in common use at Rome and throughout Italy early in the sixth century; a Council of Vaison held in 529[1] directs the dioceses of South Gaul to introduce into all their churches "the sweet and wholesome custom of frequently repeating the *Kyrie* which is prevalent throughout the East and in Italy, as well as at Rome." Rome, however, in the days of Gregory[2], had departed from the strictness of the Eastern form, varying the strain by *Christe eleison: Kyrie* and *Christe* were repeated alternately, or the choir continued to sing the *Kyrie* until a nod from the officiating bishop or priest warned them to "change the litany," when *Christe*

[1] Conc. Vas. ii. *Can.* 3.
[2] Greg. M. *Ep.* vii. 64.

took its place [1]. After a time further modifications were introduced. The threefold *Kyrie*, or a double *Kyrie* with a *Christe* intervening, seems to have suggested a formal invocation of the Holy Trinity; and, further, the simple prayer for mercy was expanded into a multitude of specific supplications. In these expansions of the original form, the Greek tongue was necessarily abandoned, and in place of *eleison* the refrains ended with *miserere nobis*, or *audi nos, parce nobis, libera nos*, "hear us," "spare us," "deliver us," as the form of the petition required.

A far more radical change in the form of the litany arose out of the growing tendency to regard the saints in the light of intercessors with God. The pious opinion of the fourth century, that the saints who were commemorated in the liturgy joined their prayers with those of the living [2], ripened into a dogma which expressed itself in a new system of devotion. The Sacramentaries abound in prayers in which God is desired to hear and answer the intercessions of His saints on behalf of the Church, and refer to

---

[1] *Ord. R.* v.
[2] Aug. *Serm.* 17.

the aid and protection afforded by particular saints to the living. It was not unnatural that those who entertained this belief should proceed to invite the help of the saints by direct invocation. The litanies, as a popular and flexible form of devotion, readily lent themselves to this practice perhaps from the time of Gregory. As early as the eighth and ninth centuries this new element in the litany threatened to overshadow the old; the *Kyrie* had almost given way to the *ora pro nobis*. Walafrid Strabo finds it necessary to explain that "the litany is not limited to the recitation of names, through which the saints are invited to the aid of human frailty[1]," and that the recitation was in fact of comparatively recent introduction. Muratori[2] prints a litany of the ninth century, of Frankish origin, in which a hundred names of saints are recited; another published by Martène contains 225[3]. It became usual to arrange the names into groups such as angels, apostles, martyrs, confessors, virgins, and the litany was known as *trina, quina, septena*, according as the number of saints under each head was three, five, or seven. In some litanies it

---

[1] *De Rebus Eccl.* 28.   [2] *Liturg. Rom. Vet.* i. 74.
[3] P. 629 f.

rose much higher; the Saxon Lenten litany commemorated twelve saints in each group; in the litany prescribed in the Pontifical of Egbert for the dedication of a church, each class contains from twenty to six-and-twenty names. Nor were the invocations restricted to Biblical saints and the greater saints of the Catholic Church; local hagiology contributed its store, and the honoured names of recently departed bishops found a place. Thus the Litany of Egbert invokes the intercession of St. Cuthbert, who died in 687, and of St. Guthlac of Crowland, whose death took place in 714, during Egbert's lifetime.

We proceed to examine the structure of a Sarum processional litany; and as one of the most perfect of its kind we will take the litany sung on Rogation Days as the procession went forth into the fields. It begins with *Kyrie eleison, Christe eleison, Christe audi nos.* Then follows the invocation of the Holy Trinity: *Pater de caelis Deus, Fili redemptor mundi Deus, Spiritus Sancte Deus, Sancta Trinitas unus Deus,* each clause followed by *miserere nobis.* Created intercessors are then invoked: (1) the Blessed Virgin; (2) Angels and Archangels, Michael, Gabriel and Raphael; (3) St. John Baptist; (4) the

Apostles and Evangelists; (5) Martyrs; (6) Confessors; (7) Virgins (twelve of each of these classes are enumerated). The "names" end with the general invocation, *Omnes sancti, orate.* Then the litany returns to the language of direct prayer: *propitius esto, parce nos, Domine.* A series of "deprecations" and "obsecrations" follows, to each of which the response is *Libera* [*nos, Domine*]; then another series of "supplications," each ending *Te rogamus.* Then follow *Agnus Dei* thrice repeated, *Kyrie eleison,* the Lord's Prayer, suffrages, and collects. The same order is observed in the Lenten litany to be found at the end of the Psalter of the Breviary, except that on the week-days of Lent each day had its own list of saints. The Easter Eve litanies used before the benediction of the font are respectively "septiform" and "quinquepartite," i.e. the saints are arranged in groups of seven in the one and of five in the other, and with the exception of a *Kyrie* at the beginning of each group, these litanies consist exclusively of such invocations.

In his original draft of the English Litany Cranmer admitted the principle of the invocation of saints, although he reduced the invocations to a minimum. Only three such clauses were admitted, the first addressed to "Saint Mary, Mother of God," the second to "all Holy Angels and Archangels," the third to "Patriarchs, Prophets, Apostles, Martyrs, Confessors, Virgins, and all the blessed company of heaven." The mediaeval litanies had always carefully preserved the distinction between prayers addressed to a Person of the Holy Trinity, and requests for intercession addressed to the angels and saints; in the latter, *ora pro nobis* had never been exceeded. Such invocations did not amount to worship even of a lower sort; but they assumed a relation between the visible and invisible sections of the Church for which there was no definite authority, and they had certainly tended to throw into obscurity the supplications offered to God. It was probably for these reasons that even the three invocations of created intercessors which appeared in 1544 were removed from the litany before its admission into the English Prayer Book of 1549. With this exception the new English Litany follows the structure of the mediaeval litanies[1].

[1] The liturgy of 1544 may be seen in an appendix to *Private Prayers put forth during the Reign of Elizabeth* (Parker Society), p. 570 f.

There is the invocation of the Holy Trinity, followed by "Spare us, good Lord;" deprecations, obsecrations, supplications, succeed in due course; then the *Agnus Dei*, the *Kyrie*, *Pater*, suffrages, and collects. As to the substance it is to a great extent the same, but compression has sometimes been used, and at other times new matter introduced, while space and time have been saved by grouping together several deprecations under one response. A literal rendering of a portion of the Sarum Litany will enable the English reader to judge for himself of the skill manifested in Cranmer's reconstruction. After the invocations the Sarum Litany proceeds:

> "From all evil,
> From the crafts of the devil,
> From everlasting damnation,
> From the imminent peril of our sins,
> From the assaults of evil spirits,
> From the spirit of fornication,
> From the desire of vainglory,
> From all uncleanness of mind and body,
> From anger, hatred, and ill-will,
> From unclean thoughts,
> From blindness of heart,
> From lightning and tempest,
> From sudden and unlooked-for death,"

each of these clauses being followed by the

words "Deliver us, Lord," repeated by the choir. Passing to the supplications we find in the Sarum Litany the following:

> "We sinners beseech Thee, hear us.
> That Thou wouldest give us peace, we beseech Thee.
> That Thou wouldest deign to govern and defend Thy holy Catholic Church, we beseech Thee;"

and so forth. In this part of the litany Cranmer has allowed himself greater liberty; the supplications have been increased in number and many of them are entirely new, suggested in several instances, there seems to be no doubt, by the Latin Litany of Hermann, the reforming Archbishop of Cologne, and by an English Litany published in Marshall's Primer nine years before the appearance of Cranmer's work. In a few instances we may regret the loss of supplications which Cranmer has omitted, e. g.—

> "That Thou wouldest deign to keep all Christian people redeemed by Thy precious Blood . . . that Thou wouldest bestow eternal blessings on our benefactors . . . that Thou wouldest enable us to offer Thee reasonable service . . . that Thou wouldest raise our minds to heavenly desires . . . that Thou wouldest grant to all the faithful departed eternal rest."

But on the whole the new series is richer and fuller than the old, and a monument of the great Archbishop's powers as a translator and reviser of ancient liturgical forms. In the suffrages and collects which follow the Lord's Prayer the Archbishop has deserted his original in favour of other ancient models which he deemed more profitable. The collect, "O God, merciful Father," is from the "Mass for sorrow of heart"; the antiphon and Psalm with the *Gloria* which strike like a burst of sunshine across the saddest part of the office, anciently preceded the Rogation-tide litany; the *preces* which follow the Psalm belonged to the Litany of St. Mark's Day and are already to be found in Egbert's Pontifical.

At the end of the English Litany is a prayer which deserves special attention, because it has been deliberately adopted from an Eastern source. The "Prayer of Chrysostome," as Cranmer called it, was doubtless believed by the Archbishop to be the work of that great bishop of the fourth century. He found it in the Liturgy attributed to St. Chrysostom, which had already been translated into Latin by Erasmus, but was apparently known to Cranmer in the original [1]. In the Liturgy of St. Chrysostom this prayer is attached to "the third antiphon," which corresponds to the Western *introit*. It is found in the same

---

[1] Burbidge, *Liturgies and Offices of the Church*, p. 41 ff.

position in the Liturgy of St. Basil[1], so that it might with equal or greater justice have been called "A Prayer of St. Basil." But the peculiar interest of the prayer as a part of the English Litany lies in the witness it bears to the learning and catholicity of the English Reformers. In Cranmer for the first time the English Church found a chief who had at once the ability and the courage to carry out the direction attributed to her founder, and to press into her service whatever was good in the worship of any Church in Christendom.

[1] See Notes, p. 223.

CHAPTER VI.

THE PONTIFICAL.

THE *pontifices* of pagan Rome were a college of priests charged with the general supervision of public and private worship. Over them was a chief pontiff, usually a public man, eminent for his services to the State. His name of office lent itself readily to the use of the Church. Tertullian, in an ironical mood, describes the Bishop of Rome as "pontifex maximus, id est, episcopus episcoporum." At a later time *pontifex* became the ordinary designation of a bishop, while the Roman bishop, when his pretensions were generally admitted in the West, acquired the style of *Pontifex pontificum*.

Thus the Pontifical (*pontificale, liber pontificalis*) is the bishop's book, i. e. the volume which supplies the bishop with the offices which belong to the episcopal ministrations. In the Middle Ages these duties were very onerous. The mediaeval bishop was not only required to confirm, ordain, and consecrate churches and churchyards; all persons or things specially dedicated to the service of GOD received his blessing. His intervention was equally needed at the benediction of an abbat or abbess, the coronation of a king or queen, the dedication of an altar, the hallowing of a cross, an image, a vestment, or a book. At the beginning and end of Lent the bishop was particularly busy: on Ash Wednesday he blessed and distributed the ashes, on the Thursday before Easter he set apart the oils for use during the ensuing year; it belonged to him also to expel the penitents and to reconcile them after their period of penance. It would be easy to add to this list of episcopal duties, but enough has been said to show that the mediaeval bishop needed a separate book of offices peculiar to his order.

In the Roman Church of the seventh and eighth centuries the forms of prayer connected with the bishop's functions were given in the Sacramentaries, while the *Ordines* supplied the ritual directions. The English Church, however, had already in the eighth century begun to collect offices and rubrics into a single volume. The Pontifical of Egbert, Archbishop of York (732–766), now preserved at Paris in a MS. of the tenth century[1], is the earliest specimen; the same library contains a MS. Pontifical of Dunstan, Archbishop of Canterbury (957–988). The Benedictional[2] of Robert of Rouen, and a Pontifical which formerly belonged to the Abbey of Jumièges, are books of the same character but of French origin.

Mr. Maskell remarks[3] that "the Pontifical of any Church is among the scarcest of its books existing." He mentions one such MS. at Bangor, three or four in the British Museum, two in the Cambridge University Library (one of them a complete copy of the Sarum Pontifical), and one at Exeter. Since 1596 the printed Roman Pontifical has superseded all local collections of the kind within the obedience of the Papal see. The Church of England has now no authorized book of offices for the use of her bishops[4]. When the English Prayer Book first appeared it contained no office requiring episcopal intervention except that of Confirmation, which took its place, as in the Manual, among parochial

---

[1] The MS. has been printed by the Surtees Society (vol. xxvii).
[2] See Maskell, *Mon. Rit.* i. p. cxxvii.   [3] *Ib.* p. cxiv.
[4] See Notes, p. 223 f.

offices for occasional use. The English Ordination services were subsequently bound up with the book, and from 1552 were permanently attached to it, although it was not till the final revision of 1661–2 that they received recognition on the title-page. Other offices used by our bishops on certain occasions, such as the Coronation service, and the orders for the Dedication of Churches and the Consecration of Churchyards and Cemeteries[1], have never gained a foothold in the Book of Common Prayer.

Thus in our present Prayer Book the Sarum Pontifical is represented only by the "Order of Confirmation" and the "Form and Manner of Making, Ordaining, and Consecrating of Bishops, Priests, and Deacons." The former has been considered in connexion with the Manual; the latter remains to be dealt with here.

In commissioning His Apostles, our Lord used the sign of insufflation, with the words, "Receive ye the Holy Ghost." It is remarkable that while the Church used insufflation at baptism, she has always shrunk from following the example of Christ in the act of ordination; even the words which accom-

[1] On these offices, see Maskell, *Mon. Rit.* iii., p. iii f.

panied the sign were not adopted before the twelfth century, and then only in the West. The Apostles themselves in sending others to any formal ministry used and required only imposition of hands and prayer [1]. This simple rite became the essential feature of ecclesiastical ordinations, giving to the ceremony its common Greek name ($\chi\epsilon\iota\rho o\theta\epsilon\tau\epsilon\hat{\iota}\nu, \chi\epsilon\iota\rho o\theta\epsilon\sigma\acute{\iota}a$). The Latin *ordinare*, whence our "ordination," signified merely to "admit into an order;" other terms used by the ancient Church point to the election of the clergy by the body of the faithful, or to their ministrations as the representatives of the Christian priesthood. But whatever the designation of the rite, it consisted both in East and West, with the rarest exceptions, in the laying on of hands accompanied by prayer. Other ceremonies grew up around this central act, but the imposition of hands, which in the course of time almost disappeared from the rite of Confirmation, has maintained its place in ordination throughout the Catholic Church [2].

The earliest forms of ordination now extant are to be found in the eighth book of the *Apostolical Constitutions*. They prescribe

[1] Acts vi. 6; 1 Tim. iv. 14, v. 22; 2 Tim. i. 6.
[2] See Gore, *Church and the Ministry*, note G., p. 383 ff.

that the deacon is to be ordained by the bishop laying hands upon him with prayer[1], and the priest in like manner, but with another form of words appropriate to his more solemn charge[2]. Directions are also given for the ordination of a deaconess, a subdeacon, and a reader[3]; in each case the office consists merely of the imposition of hands and a benediction. For the bishop there is a more elaborate ceremonial[4]. He is to be elected by the whole body, and, after election, submitted finally to the approval of the Church assembled for the worship of the Lord's day. If all agree to pronounce him "worthy," the consecration proceeds. "One of the chief bishops," standing near the altar with two other bishops, offers the Prayer of Consecration, the rest of the bishops and presbyters praying silently meanwhile, and the deacons holding the Book of the Holy Gospels open over the head of the elect. To the prayer of the consecrator the clergy and people answer "Amen," and the Eucharist is then placed in the hands of the new bishop. The next morning he takes his seat with the other bishops (ἐνθρονιζέσθω εἰς τὸν αὐτῷ διαφέροντα

[1] viii. 17, 18. [2] viii. 16.
[3] viii. 19 f.   [4] viii. 3 f.

τόπον παρὰ τῶν λοιπῶν ἐπισκόπων), receives from them all the holy kiss, preaches to his flock, and finally celebrates the holy mysteries.

It will be observed that in this earliest detailed account of a consecration no mention is made of any imposition of hands; in place of it the Book of the Gospels is held over the head of the elect while the consecrator prays. This strange omission occurs also in the forms for the consecration of the Bishops of Alexandria and Rome. At first sight it seems to be fatal to the hypothesis that the imposition of hands is essential to a valid ordination, and Dr. Hatch did not hesitate to draw that inference [1]. Another interpretation has been quite recently put upon the facts by Mr. Lacey, which deserves serious consideration [2]. The omission appears to be limited to the consecration of two or three of the greatest bishops of ancient Christendon. The Bishops of Rome and Alexandria occupied a position of eminence which seemed to entitle them to special privileges in the manner of their admission to office. A bishop elect of one of these great sees was unwilling to receive benediction from those who would

---

[1] Hatch, *Organization*, p. 133 f.
[2] Lacey, *L'Imposition des Mains*, p. 17 f.

be his inferiors. But the Book of the Gospels represented the person of Christ; when it was opened over his head it was as if Christ's own hands were laid upon him, and Christ Himself were acting as consecrator. Other Western sees followed the example so far as they dared; they added the imposition of the open Gospels, without abandoning the imposition of episcopal hands. An early instance of this may be seen in the *Statuta antiqua ecclesiae*, which are believed to represent the practice of the province of Arles in the sixth century[1]. According to these Gallican canons, when a bishop is to be consecrated, each of the consecrating bishops touches the head of the elect, one of them pronouncing the benediction, while two other bishops hold the Book of the Gospels over his head and neck.

Apart from this special feature which characterized the consecration of the Pope, in what form did the ancient Church of Rome impart orders to her clergy?

A letter written in the year 251 by Cornelius, Bishop of Rome, to Fabius, Bishop of Antioch, and preserved in the *Church History* of Eusebius[2], contains a list of the clergy of various orders then connected with the Roman

---

[1] Duchesne, *Origines*, p. 337.   [2] vi. 43.

Church. Under the Bishop of Rome there were in the middle of the third century forty-six presbyters, seven deacons, seven sub-deacons, forty-two acolytes, and fifty-two exorcists, readers, and door-keepers. For the admission of new members into these eight orders certain forms of ordination must already have existed. What they were may perhaps be gathered from the Canons of Hippolytus, which describe at length the ordering of bishops, priests, and deacons. The bishop is to be chosen by the whole Church, and at the time of his ordination a consecrator, selected from the bishops and priests, is to lay his hand on the head of the elect and offer a prescribed form of prayer; after this he receives the kiss of peace from all who are present, and the Eucharist is celebrated. The priest is similarly ordained, but he is not, like the bishop, enthroned. For the deacon another form of benediction is provided, appropriate to his inferior rank. As for the reader, he receives from the bishop the book of the Gospels, but no imposition of hands.

We are on surer ground when we reach the Roman Sacramentaries and *Ordines* of the seventh and eighth centuries. It was now the custom at Rome to limit the conferring of

Orders to the four annual fasts of the Church year. The "fasts of the four seasons" had been observed in the Roman Church from the days of Leo I, and not a few of the sermons of that great Pope were preached on these occasions. These fasts, which correspond roughly with our Ember weeks, were held in the first, fourth, seventh, and tenth months[1], i. e. in March, June, September, and December. In the time of Gelasius[2] they were already regarded as the canonical seasons of ordination. On the Thursday and Friday of these weeks the Pope or his deputy announced the names of the subdeacons or deacons belonging to any of the parishes of Rome who had been elected into the diaconate or the priesthood, and charged those who were present, if they had aught against any of the candidates, to come forward and state the objection. If no objection was alleged, the ordination followed on Saturday, at the Mass of the Vigil. After the Introit of the Mass the Pope rose and invited the prayers of the congregation for the candidates. The Litany was then sung by the *schola cantorum*, all kneeling. Then the Pope rose again, laid his hands on the head of each

[1] *Ord. Rom.* i. 33.   [2] *Ep.* 9.

candidate for the diaconate, and pronounced a prayer of consecration. After this the candidates for the priesthood advanced and were similarly ordained. The consecration of bishops was conducted with the same ritual, excepting that the election was verified, and the elect underwent an examination by the Pope before hands were laid upon him. The ordination of a bishop took place always on a Sunday.

So simple, according to M. Duchesne [1], were the Roman rites of ordination. Various traces of a more elaborate ritual which appear in the Gelasian Sacramentary [2] are ascribed by the same eminent authority to Gallican influence. In the Gallican ordination of priests as represented in the *Missale Francorum*, besides the appearance of such Eastern customs as the shout of approval, 'Dignus est,' with which the faithful respond to the bishop's inquiry, and the observance of the ritual prescribed in the *Statuta antiqua*, we find for the first time the consecration of the hands of the new priest or bishop by the use of unction and a special prayer.

The Pontifical of Egbert introduces us to the ordination services of the English Church

---

[1] *Origines*, p. 339 f.   [2] Wilson, p. xxvii.

in the eighth century. Both the liturgical forms and the ceremonial are now much fuller. Three forms of prayer are used, known as the *consecratio*, the *consummatio*, and the *benedictio*; the hands are anointed as in the Gallican ritual, unction is applied to the head of the priest and bishop; and in the case of each order the *insignia* of office are committed to the newly ordained: the deacon is vested with the stole thrown over his left shoulder; the priest has the stole placed round his neck and over both shoulders, and is invested with the chasuble; the bishop receives the pastoral staff and ring, and is seated in the episcopal chair. At the imposition of hands the early Gallican rules are observed, the deacon receiving it from the bishop alone, the priest from the bishop and the priests present, the bishop from the bishops present, while the open Gospels are held over his neck.

We may now turn to the forms in the Sarum Pontifical. On the Saturday in Ember week, after the Collect of Mass, all the candidates are presented by the archdeacon; and the bishop, having received from him assurances as to their fitness, appeals to the people to come forward if there is aught against any of them. If no objection is alleged, the ordination proceeds. First, the candidates for the minor orders are successively ordained—door-keepers, readers, exorcists, acolytes, and subdeacons. The Epistle follows the ordering of the subdeacons, and when it has been read, the candidates for the diaconate and priesthood advance and the Litany is sung; in the course of it the bishop rises, takes his pastoral staff, and, facing the candidates, offers three special supplications on their behalf. After the Litany the priests elect retire, the deacons elect remaining before the bishop. The prayers that follow are substantially those of Egbert's Pontifical, but important changes have passed over the rite since early Anglo-Saxon days. The bishop lays his hand on each deacon, saying, "Receive the Holy Ghost." The deacon is vested with the dalmatic; the Book of the Gospels is delivered to him with the words, "Receive power to read the Gospels in the Church of God, both for the living and the dead." Then the deacon who is the last to be ordained reads the Gospel, the deacons retire, and the candidates for the priesthood advance. The priest receives the stole and

hostiasque pro delictis atq; negligentiu͡ popu- /
puli offerunt. & ad cetera benedicenda q͡ /
ad usus populi necessaria sunt. & p͡ta q͡s /
ut quecumq; benedixerint benedicantur. /
& quecumq; sacrauerint sacrent͡. Saluator /
mundi. Q͡ uiuis &c. d͡s. P. Consecratio /
manuu͡ sacerdotis de oleo & chrismate. /

Consecrare & s͡cificare digneris q͡s d͡ne /
 manus istas p istam unctionem & /
n͡ram benedictionem. ut quecumq; conse /
crauerint consecrentur. & quecumq; benedi /
xerint benedicantur. & sanctificentur in no /
mine d͡ni. R. xp͡m. Deinde patenam /
cum oblatis. & calicem cum uino det /
singulis dicens ad eos lenta voce. /

Accipite potestate͡ offerre sacrificiu͡ deo. /
missamq; celebrare tam p uiuis q͡m & p /
defunctis in no͡ie d͡ni. Ad consummandu͡ /
ut nobis sit c͡oiter p͡brat' officiu͡. /

Oratio ut hi qui in adiutorium & /
utilitate͡ n͡re salutis digiunt p͡bri. bene /
dictione diuini muneris indulgentiam /

ORDERING OF PRIESTS.
WINCHESTER PONTIFICAL (CAMB. UNIV. LIB. EE. II. 3). [To face p. 204]

chasuble, as in Egbert's rite. The *Veni Creator* is sung, all kneeling, the bishop beginning. After the consecration of the hands, the paten with oblates and the chalice containing wine are put into them with the words, "Receive power to offer sacrifice to God, and to celebrate Mass both for the living and the dead." The Mass then proceeds, the bishop celebrating. Just before the *postcommunio*, the bishop again lays his hand on each of the new priests, saying, "Receive the Holy Ghost; whose sins thou dost forgive, they are forgiven, and whose sins thou dost retain, they are retained."

The consecration of a bishop elect, which in obedience to the Roman rule could take place only on a Sunday, is a rite of much complexity. Before Mass begins, the elect is examined at great length upon his readiness to perform the duties of the episcopal office, and upon his faith. After the Gradual he appears fully vested, with the exception of the mitre, the staff, and the ring, and is presented by two bishops to the archbishop of the province. The Litany is said with special supplications, after which, while two bishops hold the Book of the Gospels over the neck of the elect, all the other bishops touching his head, the consecrator begins *Veni Creator*. The head and hands of the elect are then consecrated with chrism and oil. Finally, the staff, ring, and mitre are blessed and presented to him, and the Book of the Gospels is delivered, suitable words accompanying the delivery of each of these *insignia*.

This is but an outline of the Roman, Gallican, Anglo-Saxon, and Sarum rites; but it is sufficient to show how gradually the apostolic laying on of hands gathered round it in the course of centuries the complicated ceremonial of mediaeval times. Much of the later ritual in both the Roman and the Sarum books was borrowed from Gaul; other features arose naturally out of the growing love of symbolism. Beside this accumulation of ceremonies, important changes were made between the eighth century and the thirteenth in the verbal forms of ordination; the *Veni Creator*, the *Accipe Spiritum Sanctum*, the formulas for the delivery of the *instrumenta*, were quite unknown to the Sacramentaries and even to the earlier of the Pontificals. No valid objection can be taken to these forms or ceremonies on the ground of late introduction, for it is admitted that the Church has power to ordain rites and ceremonies in addition to those of apostolic or primitive authority, provided that the additions are not inconsistent with the original rite. On the other hand, such accretions cannot fairly be held to be of the essence of the rite; or, in technical language, the "matter" and "form" of Holy Orders are not to be sought in them, still less to be restricted to them.

In the English Ordination Service annexed to the First Prayer Book, and with some important changes incorporated in our present book, there is certainly nothing like a wholesale rejection of mediaeval additions. Not only does our Ordinal follow ancient precedent in connecting the bestowal of Holy Orders with the celebration of the Holy Communion, and in its strict adherence to the old rule, long adopted throughout the West, which requires the presbyterate to join with the bishop in the laying on of hands upon a priest, and three bishops at least to take part in the consecration of a bishop; not only does the Anglican Church follow the example of the ancient Roman Church in limiting the ordination of deacons and priests to the four annual seasons of fasting and prayer, and the consecration of a bishop to Sundays or holy days; not only do the prayers of the Ordination Service rest ultimately on the ancient forms; but we have retained such late additions as the *Veni Creator* and the *Accipe Spiritum Sanctum*, and the delivery of a book as the sign of office. On the other hand, we have abandoned, as in Baptism and Confirmation, the use of unction; we no longer practise the formal vesting of the ordinands, or the use of the words which assigned to the priest the power of offering sacrifice; and since 1552 we have ceased to deliver the chalice to the priest or the pastoral staff to the bishop.

Whatever may be thought of the expediency of these omissions, there is no reason for suspecting that they affect the validity of Orders conferred after the English rite [1]. Ceremonies which were unknown to the Church of the first three centuries and are still unknown to the Eastern Church cannot be essential to the act of ordination. As to the forms, no particular words have come down to us invested with apostolical or Catholic authority; it is sufficient that prayer should accompany or precede the imposition of hands.

[1] On this question the reader may consult with advantage Bp. J. Wordsworth, *De Validitate Ordinum Anglicanorum*, p. 18 ff.; or E. Denny and T. A. Lacey, *De Hierarchia Anglicana Dissertatio Apologetica* cc. 3, 5.

No early forms of ordination include a delivery of the *instrumenta*, or the words "Receive the power of offering sacrifice." The English priest receives the Holy Ghost "for the office and work of a priest in the Church of God," and the words include all the functions which belong to his order, whatever they may be. On the other hand, it is not maintained that the words which we use at the ordering of priests are indispensable. We have omitted the *Accipe Spiritum Sanctum* in the making of deacons [1]; if we retain it in the conferring of the higher order, it is because these words of Christ seemed to our Reformers the most appropriate which could be used at that solemn moment, and the most suggestive of the source from which the priest may look for strength. No words could so well impress upon him the profound truth that "whether we preach, pray, baptize, communicate, condemn, give absolution, or whatsoever, as disposers of GOD's mysteries, our words, judgements, acts, and deeds are not ours, but the Holy Ghost's [2]."

[1] Comp. Churton, *On the English Ordinal*, p. 19.
[2] Hooker, *E. P.* v. 77, § 8.

NOTES.

PAGE 9.

Bede, *H. E.* i. 27. *Interrogatio Augustini.* Cum una sit fides, sunt ecclesiarum diversae consuetudines, et altera consuetudo missarum in sancta Romana ecclesia, atque altera in Galliarum tenetur. *Respondit Gregorius papa.* Novit fraternitas tua Romanae ecclesiae consuetudinem, in qua se meminit nutritam. Sed mihi placet, sive in Romana, sive in Galliarum, seu in qualibet ecclesia, aliquid invenisti quod plus omnipotenti Deo possit placere, sollicite eligas, et in Anglorum ecclesia, quae adhuc ad fidem nova est, institutione praecipua, quae de multis ecclesiis colligere potuisti, infundas. Non enim pro locis res, sed pro bonis rebus loca amanda sunt. Ex singulis ergo quibusque ecclesiis, quae pia, quae religiosa, quae recta sunt elige, et haec quasi in fasciculum collecta, apud Anglorum mentes in consuetudinem depone.

PAGE 19.

Besides the Canonical Hours the mediaeval Church observed Hours in honour of the Blessed Virgin Mary, known as the "little office." Originally a monastic devotion, these Hours were by a canon of the Council of Clermont in 1098 made obligatory on the secular clergy, and eventually became popular with the laity. The richly illuminated *Horae*, so conspicuous in all collections of mediaeval MSS., are of this type. Other devotional matter gathered round the Hours of the Virgin, just as in the case of the Breviary, and the *Horae B..V. Mariae secundum usum Sarum* had its kalendar, its penitential and gradual psalms, its litany, and especially the Vigils of the Dead, the *Dirige* and *Placebo*, and the 'Commendation.' In this fuller form the *Horae* became the prayer-book of the educated laity, and the wealthy procured copies for their own use, written oftentimes in a minute hand, and adorned with exquisite vignettes and marginal decorations.

The *Horae* formed the basis of an English book which to some extent prepared the laity for the rendering of the services into the mother tongue. The English 'Hours' were known as the Prymer, or Primer, and several MSS. of this kind have survived from the fourteenth and fifteenth centuries. Specimens may be seen in Mr. Maskell's *Monumenta Ritualia*, vol. ii. (=iii. ed. 1882); the Early English Text Society has recently published the text of a Prymer c. 1420-30 A.D. preserved in the Cambridge University Library (London, 1895).

PAGE 34.

Basil, *Epp.* ii. 207. Τὰ νῦν κεκρατηκότα ἔθη πάσαις ταῖς τοῦ θεοῦ ἐκκλησίαις συνῳδά ἐστι καὶ σύμφωνα. ἐκ νυκτὸς γὰρ ὀρθρίζει παρ' ἡμῖν ὁ λαὸς ἐπὶ τὸν οἶκον τῆς προσευχῆς καὶ ἐν πόνῳ καὶ θλίψει καὶ συνοχῇ δακρύων ἐξομολογούμενοι τῷ θεῷ, τελευταῖον ἐξαναστάντες τῶν προσευχῶν εἰς τὴν ψαλμῳδίαν καθίστανται. καὶ νῦν μὲν διχῇ διανεμηθέντες ἀντιψάλλουσιν ἀλλήλοις· . . . ἔπειτα πάλιν ἐπιτρέψαντες ἑνὶ κατάρχειν τοῦ μέλους, οἱ λοιποὶ ὑπηχοῦσι· καὶ οὕτως ἐν τῇ ποικιλίᾳ τῆς ψαλμῳδίας τὴν νύκτα διενεγκόντες, μεταξὺ προσευχόμενοι, ἡμέρας ἤδη ὑπολαμπούσης, πάντες κοινῇ ὡς ἐξ ἑνὸς στόματος καὶ μιᾶς καρδίας τὸν τῆς ἐξομολογήσεως ψαλμὸν ἀναφέρουσι τῷ κυρίῳ.

PAGE 35.

Silviae Peregr., ed. 2, 1888, p. 45. Singulis diebus ante pullorum cantum aperiuntur omnia hostia Anastasis, et descendent omnes monazontes et parthenae, ut hic dicunt, et non solum hii, sed et laici praeterea, viri aut mulieres, qui tamen volunt maturius vigilare; et ex ea hora usque in lucem dicuntur ymni et psalmi respondentur, similiter et antiphonae; et cata singulos ymnos fit oratio. Nam presbyteri bini vel terni, similiter et diacones, singulis diebus vices habent simul cum monazontes, qui cata singulos ymnos vel antiphonas orationes dicunt. Iam autem ubi ceperit lucescere, tunc incipiunt matutinos hymnos dicere; ecce et supervenit episcopus cum clero, et statim ingreditur intro spelunca et de intro cancellos primum dicet orationem pro omnibus; commemorat etiam ipse nomina quorum vult, sic benedicet cathecuminos. Item dicet orationem et benedicet fideles ... Hora autem decima (quod appellant hic licinicon [τὸ λυχνικόν], nam nos dicimus "lucernare") similiter se omnis multitudo colliget ad Anastasim, incenduntur omnes candelae et cerei, et fit lumen infinitum ... dicuntur etiam psalmi lucernares, sed et antiphonas diutius ... et diacono dicente singulorum nomina semper pisinni plurimi stant respondentes semper *Kyrie eleyson* ... dicet episcopus stans benedictionem super cathecuminos ... item benedicet fideles episcopus, et sic fit missa Anastasi.

PAGE 44.

Bede, *H. E.* i. 26. Erat autem prope ipsam civitatem ad orientem ecclesia in honorem sancti Martini antiquitus facta dum adhuc Romani Brittaniam incolerent, in qua regina, quam Christianam fuisse praediximus, orare consueverat. In hac ergo et ipsi primo convenire, psallere, orare, missas facere, praedicare, et baptizare coeperunt; donec rege ad fidem converso maiorem praedicandi per omnia et ecclesias fabricandi vel restaurandi licentiam acciperent.

PAGE 45.

Bede, *H. E.* iv. 18. Accepit et praefatum Iohannem abbatem Brittaniam perducendum, quatenus in monasterio suo cursum canendi annuum, sicut ad sanctum Petrum Romae agebatur, edoceret; egitque abba Iohannes ut iussionem acceperat pontificis, et ordinem videlicet, ritumque canendi ac legendi viva voce praefati monasterii cantores edocendo, et ea quae totius anni circulus in celebratione dierum festorum poscebat etiam litteris mandando. Quae hactenus in eodem monasterio servata et a multis iam sunt circumquaque transscripta. Non solum autem idem Iohannes ipsius monasterii fratres docebat, verum de omnibus pene eiusdem provinciae monasteriis ad audiendum eum qui cantandi erant periti confluebant; sed et ipsum per loca, in quibus doceret, multi invitare curabant.

PAGE 74.

Professor Skeat has favoured me with the following luminous account of the process by which *missa* has passed into the English *mass*. "There were two pronunciations of Latin, the one polite, the other vulgar, in the early centuries after A.D. 400. The polite Latin *ĭ* is always *ĕ* in Folk-Latin, which is the real source of the Romance languages ... for example, for *viridem* the Folk-Latin had *ver'dem*, which is the source of Ital. *verde*, French *vert*, &c. ... In Italian the Latin *mittere* is *mettere* ... Hence came Ital. *messa*; French *messe*; Old High German, *messe*; early Anglo-Saxon *messe* ... The later A.S. form became *mæsse* (with *æ* as in *cat*, and final *e* sounded). This was respelt by French scribes (temp. Edw. I) as *masse*, and hence not only modern English *mass*, but *-mas* as a suffix. This change from Latin *i*, through *e*, to English *a*, is rare; but there is a case not very unlike; the Lat. *mirabilia*, neut. pl., became fem. sing. in French as *merveille*, and hence we have *marvel* in English. But here the *e* became *a* owing to the following *r*: cf. *varmin*,' *Varsity* ... The A.S. *messe* must have come in with St. Augustine, about A.D. 600. But already, by A.D. 500, the Folk-Latin was in the ascendant. This seems to explain the matter sufficiently." In another letter Professor Skeat adds: "The earliest quotation I can find for the A.S. form *messe* is in a Canterbury charter of Oswulf (805–831), printed by Kemble (i. 293), and in Thorpe's *Diplomatarium*, p. 461, and Sweet's *Oldest English Texts*, p. 444. But it must have been known in the seventh century."

PAGE 78.

Didache, c. 9, 10, 14 Περὶ δὲ τῆς εὐχαριστίας, οὕτω εὐχαριστήσατε. πρῶτον περὶ τοῦ ποτηρίου· Εὐχαριστοῦμέν σοι, πάτερ ἡμῶν, ὑπὲρ τῆς ἁγίας ἀμπέλου Δαυὶδ τοῦ παιδός σου ἧς ἐγνώρισας ἡμῖν διὰ Ἰησοῦ τοῦ παιδός σου· σοὶ ἡ δόξα εἰς τοὺς αἰῶνας. περὶ δὲ τοῦ κλάσματος· Εὐχαριστοῦμέν σοι, πάτερ ἡμῶν, ὑπὲρ τῆς ζωῆς καὶ γνώσεως ἧς ἐγνώρισας ἡμῖν διὰ Ἰησοῦ τοῦ παιδός σου· σοὶ ἡ δόξα εἰς τοὺς αἰῶνας. ὥσπερ ἦν τοῦτο κλάσμα διεσκορπισμένον ἐπάνω τῶν ὀρέων καὶ συναχθὲν ἐγένετο ἕν, οὕτω συναχθήτω σου ἡ ἐκκλησία ἀπὸ τῶν περάτων τῆς γῆς εἰς τὴν σὴν βασιλείαν· ὅτι

σοῦ ἐστιν ἡ δόξα καὶ ἡ δύναμις διὰ Ἰησοῦ Χριστοῦ εἰς τοὺς αἰῶνας.
μηδεὶς δὲ φαγέτω μηδὲ πιέτε ἀπὸ τῆς εὐχαριστίας ὑμῶν, ἀλλ᾽ οἱ
βαπτισθέντες εἰς ὄνομα Κυρίου· καὶ γὰρ περὶ τούτου εἴρηκεν ὁ
κύριος Μὴ δῶτε τὸ ἅγιον τοῖς κυσί. μετὰ δὲ τὸ ἐμπλησθῆναι
οὕτως εὐχαριστήσατε. Εὐχαριστοῦμέν σοι, πάτερ ἅγιε, ὑπὲρ
τοῦ ἁγίου ὀνόματός σου οὗ κατεσκήνωσας ἐν ταῖς καρδίαις ἡμῶν,
καὶ ὑπὲρ τῆς γνώσεως καὶ πίστεως καὶ ἀθανασίας ἧς ἐγνώρισας
ἡμῖν διὰ Ἰησοῦ τοῦ παιδός σου· σοὶ ἡ δόξα εἰς τοὺς αἰῶνας. Σύ,
δέσποτα παντόκρατορ, ἔκτισας τὰ πάντα ἕνεκεν τοῦ ὀνόματός σου·
τροφήν τε καὶ ποτὸν ἔδωκας τοῖς ἀνθρώποις εἰς ἀπόλαυσιν, ἵνα σοι
εὐχαριστήσωσιν, ἡμῖν τε ἐχαρίσω πνευματικὴν τροφὴν καὶ ποτὸν
καὶ ζωὴν αἰώνιον διὰ τοῦ παιδός σου. πρὸ πάντων εὐχαριστοῦμέν
σοι ὅτι δυνατὸς εἶ· σοὶ ἡ δόξα εἰς τοὺς αἰῶνας. μνήσθητι, Κύριε,
τῆς ἐκκλησίας σου τοῦ ῥύσασθαι αὐτὴν ἀπὸ παντὸς πονηροῦ
καὶ τελειῶσαι αὐτὴν ἐν τῇ ἀγάπῃ σου, καὶ σύναξον αὐτὴν ἀπὸ τῶν
τεσσάρων ἀνέμων, τὴν ἁγιασθεῖσαν εἰς τὴν σὴν βασιλείαν ἣν ἡτοί-
μασας αὐτῇ· ὅτι σοῦ ἐστιν ἡ δύναμις καὶ ἡ δόξα εἰς τοὺς αἰῶνας.
Ἐλθέτω χάρις, καὶ παρελθέτω ὁ κόσμος οὗτος. Ὡσαννὰ τῷ θεῷ
Δαυίδ. Εἴ τις ἅγιός ἐστιν, ἐρχέσθω· εἴ τις οὐκ ἔστι, μετανοείτω.
Μαραναθά, ἀμήν. τοῖς δὲ προφήταις ἐπιτρέπετε εὐχαριστεῖν ὅσα
θέλουσιν ... κατὰ κυριακὴν δὲ Κυρίου συναχθέντες κλάσατε ἄρτον,
καὶ εὐχαριστήσατε προεξομολογησάμενοι τὰ παραπτώματα ὑμῶν,
ἵνα καθαρὰ ἡ θυσία ἡμῶν ᾖ. πᾶς δὲ ἔχων τὴν ἀμφιβολίαν μετὰ
τοῦ ἑταίρου αὐτοῦ μὴ συνελθέτω ὑμῖν ἕως οὗ διαλλαγῶσιν, ἵνα μὴ
κοινωθῇ ἡ θυσία ὑμῶν· αὕτη γάρ ἐστιν ἡ ῥηθεῖσα ὑπὸ Κυρίου Ἐν
παντὶ τόπῳ καὶ χρόνῳ προσφέρειν μοι θυσίαν καθαράν.

Page 82.

Justin Martyr, *Apol.* i. 65, 67.

Ἡμεῖς δὲ μετὰ τὸ οὕτως
λοῦσαι τὸν πεπεισμένον καὶ
συγκατατεθειμένον ἐπὶ τοὺς
λεγομένους ἀδελφοὺς ἄγομεν,
ἔνθα συνηγμένοι εἰσί, κοινὰς
εὐχὰς ποιησόμενοι ... ἀλλήλους
φιλήματι ἀσπαζόμεθα παυσά-
μενοι τῶν εὐχῶν. ἔπειτα προσφέρεται τῷ προεστῶτι τῶν
ἀδελφῶν ἄρτος καὶ ποτήριον
ὕδατος καὶ κράματος, καὶ οὗτος

Καὶ τῇ τοῦ ἡλίου λεγομένῃ
ἡμέρᾳ πάντων κατὰ πόλεις ἢ
ἀγροὺς μενόντων ἐπὶ τὸ αὐτὸ
συνέλευσις γίνεται, καὶ τὰ ἀπο-
μνημονεύματα τῶν ἀποστόλων
ἢ τὰ συγγράμματα τῶν προ-
φητῶν ἀναγινώσκεται μέχρις
ἐγχωρεῖ. Εἶτα παυσαμένου τοῦ
ἀναγινώσκοντος ὁ προεστὼς διὰ
λόγου τὴν νουθεσίαν καὶ πρόκ-
κλησιν τῆς τῶν καλῶν τούτων

λαβὼν οἶνον καὶ δόξαν τῷ πατρὶ τῶν ὅλων διὰ τοῦ ὀνόματος τοῦ υἱοῦ καὶ τοῦ πνεύματος τοῦ ἁγίου ἀναπέμπει καὶ εὐχαριστίαν ὑπὲρ τοῦ κατηξιῶσθαι τούτων παρ' αὐτοῦ ἐπὶ πολὺ ποιεῖται. οὗ συντελέσαντος τὰς εὐχὰς καὶ τὴν εὐχαριστίαν πᾶς ὁ παρὼν λαὸς ἐπευφημεῖ λέγων 'Αμήν... εὐχαριστήσαντος δὲ τοῦ προεστῶτος καὶ ἐπευφημήσαντος παντὸς τοῦ λαοῦ οἱ καλούμενοι παρ' ἡμῖν διάκονοι διδόασιν ἑκάστῳ τῶν παρόντων μεταλαβεῖν ἀπὸ τοῦ εὐχαριστηθέντος ἄρτου καὶ οἴνου καὶ ὕδατος, καὶ τοῖς οὐ παροῦσιν ἀποφέρουσι.

μιμήσεως ποιεῖται. ἔπειτα ἀνιστάμεθα κοινῇ πάντες καὶ εὐχὰς πέμπομεν· καὶ ὡς προέφημεν, παυσαμένων ἡμῶν τῆς εὐχῆς ἄρτος προσφέρεται καὶ οἶνος καὶ ὕδωρ, καὶ ὁ προεστὼς εὐχὰς ὁμοίως καὶ εὐχαριστίας, ὅση δύναμις αὐτῷ, ἀναπέμπει, καὶ ὁ λαὸς ἐπευφημεῖ λέγων τὸ 'Αμήν' καὶ ἡ διάδοσις καὶ ἡ μετάληψις ἀπὸ τῶν εὐχαριστηθέντων ἑκάστῳ γίνεται, καὶ τοῖς οὐ παροῦσι διὰ τῶν διακόνων πέμπεται.

Page 85.

Cyril Hier. *Cat. Myst.* v Ἑωράκατε τοίνυν τὸν διάκονον τὸν νίψασθαι διδόντα τῷ ἱερεῖ καὶ τοῖς κυκλοῦσι τὸ θυσιαστήριον τοῦ θεοῦ πρεσβυτέροις... εἶτα βοᾷ ὁ διάκονος 'Αλλήλους ἀπολάβετε, καὶ ἀλλήλους ἀσπαζώμεθα... μετὰ τοῦτο βοᾷ ὁ ἱερεύς Ἄνω τὰς καρδίας... εἶτα ἀποκρίνεσθε Ἔχομεν πρὸς τὸν κύριον... εἶτα ὁ ἱερεὺς λέγει Εὐχαριστήσωμεν τῷ κυρίῳ... εἶτα λέγετε Ἄξιον καὶ δίκαιον. μετὰ ταῦτα μνημονεύομεν οὐρανοῦ καὶ γῆς [the Preface and Sanctus]. εἶτα... παρακαλοῦμεν τὸν φιλάνθρωπον θεὸν τὸ ἅγιον πνεῦμα ἐξαποστεῖλαι ἐπὶ τὰ προκείμενα ἵνα ποιήσῃ τὸν μὲν ἄρτον σῶμα Χριστοῦ τὸν δὲ οἶνον αἷμα Χριστοῦ... εἶτα... παρακαλοῦμεν τὸν θεὸν ὑπὲρ κοινῆς τῶν ἐκκλησιῶν εἰρήνης... καὶ ἁπαξαπλῶς ὑπὲρ πάντων βοηθείας δεομένων δεόμεθα πάντες ἡμεῖς καὶ ταύτην προσφέρομεν τὴν θυσίαν. εἶτα μνημονεύομεν τῶν προκεκοιμημένων... εἶτα μετὰ ταῦτα τὴν εὐχὴν λέγομεν ἣν ὁ σωτὴρ παρέδωκε τοῖς οἰκείοις αὐτοῦ μαθηταῖς... εἶτα μετὰ τὴν πλήρωσιν τῆς εὐχῆς λέγεις 'Αμήν... μετὰ ταῦτα λέγει ὁ ἱερεύς Τὰ ἅγια τοῖς ἁγίοις... εἶτα ὑμεῖς λέγετε Εἷς ἅγιος, εἷς κύριος, Ἰησοῦς Χριστός... μετὰ ταῦτα ἀκούετε τοῦ ψάλλοντος μετὰ μέλους θείου προτρεπομένου ὑμᾶς εἰς τὴν κοινωνίαν τῶν ἁγίων μυστηρίων καὶ λέγοντος Γεύσασθε καὶ ἴδετε ὅτι χρηστὸς ὁ κύριος... [The communicant receives λέγων τὸ 'Αμήν. The final direction is: ἀναμείνας τὴν εὐχὴν εὐχαρίστει τῷ θεῷ τῷ καταξιώσαντί σε τῶν τηλικούτων μυστηρίων].

Page 91.

The following fragment of a Gallican Mass for Christmas Eve was found some years ago in the library of Gonville and Caius College, on a leaf written in the eighth century, and pasted into the binding of a later MS.

[Collectio post Sanctus.]

Misericors qui nescientibus fuisti misertor per Christum Dominum nostrum, qui pridie quam pateretur...

Collectio post Secreta.

Deus qui hanc sacratissimam noctem per beatae Mariae sacrae uirginis partum sine humana concupiscentia procreatum ueri luminis fecisti inlustratione clarescere; da nobis, quaesumus, ut cuius lucis mysterium in terra cognouimus, eius quoque gaudiis in caelo perfruamur. Ex his quoque sacris libaminibus odor ad te suauitatis ascendat, atque in his benedictio a te copiosa descendat, ut per mysterium tuae operationis fiat nobis eucharistia legitima et uerus sanguis. in nomine patris et filii et spiritus sancti in saecula saeculorum.

Collectio ante Orationem.

Totis sensibus hodiernum, Domine, sacrificium celebramus quo nobis ipsius sacrificii sunt nata primordia, per eundem dominum nostrum Iesum Christum cuius orantes uerba recitamus dicentes *Pater*.

Collectio post Orationem.

Libera nos omnipotens Deus ab omnibus malis, et praesta ut natus hac nocte Saluator mundi, sicut diuinae nobis generationis est auctor ita et inmortalitatis sit ipse largitor, quod ipse praestet.

Benedictio Populi.

Populum tuum, quaesumus, Domine, pio fauore prosequere, pro quo dignatus es in hac sacratissima nocte tuam mundo praesentiam exhibere ✠ ✠ ✠ A cunctis eum aduersitatibus paterna pietate custodi, pro quo in mundo hoc tempore ex uirgine dignatus es nasci; ut in te semper exultans redemptionis suae principale munus intellegat et tua uera....

PAGE 118. The following table will show the narrative form, as compared with

S. JAMES[1].	GELASIAN[2].
Ἐν τῇ νυκτὶ ᾗ παρεδίδοτο, μᾶλλον δὲ ἑαυτὸν παρεδίδου, ὑπὲρ τῆς τοῦ κόσμου ζωῆς, λαβὼν ἄρτον ἐπὶ τῶν ἁγίων καὶ ἀχράντων καὶ ἀθανάτων αὐτοῦ χειρῶν, ἀναβλέψας εἰς τὸν οὐρανὸν καὶ ἀναδείξας σοὶ τῷ θεῷ καὶ πατρὶ καὶ εὐχαριστήσας, εὐλογήσας, ἁγιάσας, κλάσας, μετέδωκε τοῖς ἁγίοις καὶ μακαρίοις αὐτοῦ μαθηταῖς καὶ ἀποστόλοις εἰπών Λάβετε, φάγετε· τοῦτό μού ἐστι τὸ σῶμα, τὸ ὑπὲρ ὑμῶν κλώμενον καὶ διαδιδόμενον εἰς ἄφεσιν ἁμαρτιῶν. ὡσαύτως μετὰ τὰ δειπνῆσαι λαβὼν ποτήριον κεκραμένον ἐξ οἴνου καὶ ὕδατος, ἀναβλέψας ... πλήσας πνεύματος ἁγίου μετέδωκε ... Πίετε ἐξ αὐτοῦ πάντες· τοῦτό μού ἐστι τὸ αἷμα, τὸ τῆς καινῆς διαθήκης, τὸ ὑπὲρ ὑμῶν καὶ πολλῶν ἐκχυνόμενον καὶ διαδιδόμενον εἰς ἄφεσιν ἁμαρτιῶν. τοῦτο ποιεῖτε εἰς τὴν ἐμὴν ἀνάμνησιν· ὁσάκις γὰρ ἐὰν ἐσθίητε τὸν ἄρτον τοῦτον καὶ τὸ ποτήριον τοῦτο πίνητε, τὸν θάνατον τοῦ υἱοῦ τοῦ ἀνθρώπου καταγγέλλετε καὶ τὴν ἀνάστασιν αὐτοῦ ὁμολογεῖτε, ἄχρις οὗ ἔλθῃ.	Qui pridie quam pateretur accepit panem in sanctas ac venerabiles manus suas elevatis oculis in caelum ad te Deum patrem suum omnipotentem, tibi gratias agens, benedixit, fregit, dedit discipulis suis dicens, Accipite et manducate ex hoc omnes : hoc est enim corpus meum. Simili modo posteaquam coenatum est, accipiens et hunc praeclarum calicem in sanctas ac venerabiles manus suas, item tibi gratias agens, benedixit, dedit discipulis suis dicens, Accipite et bibite ex eo omnes : hic est enim calix sanguinis mei novi et aeterni testamenti, mysterium fidei, qui pro vobis et pro multis effundetur in remissionem peccatorum. Haec quotiescunque feceritis in mei memoriam facietis.

[1] So, with verbal changes, St. Mark, St. Basil, St. Chrysostom, &c.

[2] So Sarum, and all liturgies of the Roman family.

of the Institution in its ancient liturgical that of the English order:

PAGE 118.

MOZARABIC.	ENGLISH (1549).
Dominus noster Iesus Christus in qua nocte tradebatur accepit panem, et gratias agens benedixit ac fregit, deditque discipulis suis dicens, Accipite et manducate : hoc est corpus meum quod pro vobis tradetur ; quotiescunque manducaveritis, hoc facite in meam commemorationem. Similiter et calicem postquam coenavit dicens, Hic est calix novi testamenti in meo sanguine qui pro vobis et pro multis effundetur in remissionem peccatorum ; quotiescunque biberitis, hoc facite in meam commemorationem. Quotiescunque manducaveritis panem hunc et calicem istam biberitis, mortem Domini annuntiabitis donec ueniat.	Who in the same night that he was betrayed, took bread, and when he had blessed and given thanks, he brake it and gave it to his disciples, saying : Take, eat, this is my body which is given for you ; do this in remembrance of me. Likewise after supper he took the cup, and when he had given thanks, he gave it to them, saying : Drink ye all of this, for this is my blood of the new testament, which is shed for you and for many, for remission of sins : do this as oft as you shall drink it, in remembrance of me.

Gasquet and Bishop (p. 444) maintain that the English form is due to Lutheran sources and not directly to the Mozarabic. On the other hand there seems to be some probability that Cranmer had formed an independent acquaintance with the edition of the Mozarabic missal published by Cardinal Ximenes A.D. 1500; see Burbidge, p. 175, ff.

PAGE 119.

The Invocation in 1549 was as follows:
"Hear us (O merciful Father) we beseech thee; and with thy holy Spirit and word vouchsafe to bless and sanctify these thy gifts and creatures of bread and wine that they may be unto us the body and blood of thy most dearly beloved Son Jesus Christ."
It immediately preceded the Narrative of the Institution.

PAGE 125.

Didache, c. 7 Περὶ δὲ τοῦ βαπτίσματος οὕτω βαπτίσατε. ταῦτα πάντα προειπόντες βαπτίσατε εἰς τὸ ὄνομα τοῦ πατρὸς καὶ τοῦ υἱοῦ καὶ τοῦ ἁγίου πνεύματος ἐν ὕδατι ζῶντι· ἐὰν δὲ μὴ ἔχῃς ὕδωρ ζῶν, εἰς ἄλλο ὕδωρ βάπτισον· εἰ δ' οὐ δύνασαι ἐν ψυχρῷ, ἐν θερμῷ· ἐὰν δὲ ἀμφότερα μὴ ἔχῃς, ἔκχεον εἰς τὴν κεφαλὴν τρὶς ὕδωρ εἰς ὄνομα πατρὸς καὶ υἱοῦ καὶ ἁγίου πνεύματος. πρὸ δὲ τοῦ βαπτίσματος προνηστευσάτω ὁ βαπτίζων καὶ ὁ βαπτιζόμενος, καὶ εἴ τινες ἄλλοι δύνανται, κελεύεις δὲ νηστεῦσαι τὸν βαπτιζόμενον πρὸ μιᾶς ἢ δύο.

PAGE 125.

Justin M. *Apol.* i. 61 Ὅσοι ἂν πεισθῶσι καὶ πιστεύωσιν ἀληθῆ ταῦτα τὰ ὑφ' ἡμῶν διδασκόμενα καὶ λεγόμενα εἶναι, καὶ βιοῦν οὕτως δύνασθαι ὑπισχνῶνται, εὔχεσθαί τε καὶ αἰτεῖν νηστεύοντες παρὰ τοῦ θεοῦ τῶν προημαρτημένων ἄφεσιν διδάσκονται, ἡμῶν συνευχομένων καὶ συννηστευόντων αὐτοῖς. ἔπειτα ἄγονται ὑφ' ἡμῶν ἔνθα ὕδωρ ἐστί, καὶ τρόπον ἀναγεννήσεως ὃν καὶ ἡμεῖς αὐτοὶ ἀνεγεννήθημεν ἀναγεννῶνται· ἐπ' ὀνόματος γὰρ τοῦ πατρὸς τῶν ὅλων καὶ δεσπότου θεοῦ καὶ τοῦ σωτῆρος ἡμῶν Ἰησοῦ Χριστοῦ καὶ πνεύματος ἁγίου τὸ ἐν τῷ ὕδατι τότε λουτρὸν ποιοῦνται... καλεῖται δὲ τοῦτο τὸ λουτρὸν φωτισμός, ὡς φωτιζομένων τὴν διάνοιαν τῶν ταῦτα μανθανόντων.

PAGE 126.

Tertullian, *de Baptismo*, 19; *de Coron. Mil.* 4; *de Bapt.* 7, 8; *Res. Carn.* 8. Diem baptismo solemniorem pascha praestat... exinde pentecoste ordinandis lavacris laetissimum spatium est. ceterum omnis dies Domini est, omnis hora, omne tempus habile baptismo ... aquam adituri ibidem sed et aliquanto prius in ecclesia sub antistitis manu contestamur nos renuntiare diabolo et pompae et angelis eius. Dehinc ter mergitamur, amplius aliquid respondentes quam Dominus in evangelio determinavit. Inde suscepti lactis et mellis concordiam praegustamus ... exinde egressi de lavacro perungimur benedicta unctione ... dehinc manus imponitur, per benedictionem advocans et invitans spiritum sanctum ... Caro abluitur ut anima emaculetur; caro ungitur, ut anima consecretur; caro signatur, ut et anima muniatur; caro manus impositione adumbratur, ut et anima spiritu illuminetur.

Page 128.

Cyril. Hieros. *Cat. Myst.* i. 2 ff.—ii. Εἰσῄειτε πρῶτον εἰς τὸν προαύλιον τοῦ βαπτιστηρίου οἶκον, καὶ πρὸς τὰς δυσμὰς ἑστῶτες ἠκούσατε καὶ προσετάττεσθε ἐκτείνειν τὴν χεῖρα, καὶ ... ὡς πρὸς παρόντα εἰπεῖν Ἀποτάσσομαί σοι, Σατανᾶ, καὶ πᾶσι τοῖς ἔργοις σου ... καὶ πάσῃ τῇ πομπῇ [σου], καὶ πάσῃ τῇ λατρείᾳ σου. ὅτε οὖν τῷ Σατανᾷ ἀποτάττῃ ... ἀνοίγεταί σοι ὁ παράδεισος τοῦ θεοῦ ... καὶ τούτου σύμβολον τὸ στραφῆναί σε ἀπὸ δυσμῶν πρὸς ἀνατολήν, τοῦ φωτὸς τὸ χωρίον. τότε σοι ἐλέγετο εἰπεῖν Πιστεύω εἰς τὸν πατέρα καὶ εἰς τὸν υἱὸν καὶ εἰς τὸ ἅγιον πνεῦμα καὶ εἰς ἓν βάπτισμα μετανοίας. καὶ ταῦτα ἐν τῷ ἐξωτέρῳ ἐγένετο οἴκῳ ... εὐθὺς οὖν εἰσελθόντες ἀπεδύεσθε τὸν χιτῶνα ... εἶτα ἀποδυθέντες ἐλαίῳ ἠλείφεσθε ἐπορκιστῷ ... μετὰ ταῦτα ἐπὶ τὴν ἁγίαν τοῦ θείου βαπτίσματος ἐχειραγωγεῖσθε κολυμβήθραν ... καὶ ἠρωτᾶτο ἕκαστος εἰ πιστεύει εἰς τὸ ὄνομα τοῦ πατρὸς καὶ τοῦ υἱοῦ καὶ τοῦ ἁγίου πνεύματος· καὶ ὡμολογήσατε τὴν σωτήριον ὁμολογίαν, καὶ κατέδυετε τρίτον εἰς τὸ ὕδωρ καὶ ἀνεδύετε πάλιν ... καὶ ὑμῖν ἀναβεβηκόσιν ἐκ τῆς κολυμβήθρας ... ἐδόθη χρίσμα ... καὶ πρῶτον ἐχρίεσθε ἐπὶ τὸ μέτωπον ... εἶτα ἐπὶ τὰ ὦτα ... εἶτα ἐπὶ τὴν ὄσφρησιν ... · μετὰ ταῦτα ἐπὶ τὰ στήθη.

Page 144.

The following clauses occur in the Mozarabic benediction of the font:

"Sepeliatur hic ille Adam vetus, resurgat novus. ℟. Amen.

"Moriatur hic omne quod carnis est; resurgat omne quod est spiritus. ℟. Amen.

"Quicunque hic renuntiant diabolo, des eis triumphare de mundo. ℞. Amen.

"Ut per ministerium nostrum tibi consecratus, aeternis ad virtutibus, aeternis praemiis consecretur. ℞. Amen."

PAGE 152.

The following are the forms printed by Maskell:

"I N. take the N. to my wedded wyf to haue and to holde fro this day forwarde for better: for wors: for richere: for poorer: in sykenesse and in hele: tyl dethe vs departe if holy chyrche it woll ordeyne, and therto I plight the my trouthe.'

"I N. take the N. to my wedded housbonder to haue and to holde fro this day forwarde for better: for wors: for richer: for poorer: in sykenesse and in hele: to be bonere and buxum in bedde and at the borde tyll dethe us departhe if holy chyrche it wol ordeyne and therto I plight the my trouthe.'

"With this rynge, I the wed, and this gold and silver I the geue, and with my body I the worshipe, and with all my wordely cathel I the endowe, In Nomine," &c.

PAGE 161.

Maskell prints a form from a MS. in the library of St. John's College, Oxford; it exists also in a Cambridge MS., and was probably widely known and used by our mediaeval parish priests. It begins and ends thus:

"My dere sone in God, thou hiest fast thi wai to Godward; there thou shalt see alle thi former faderis, apostils, martiris, confessoris, virginis, and alle men and wommen that be sauid ... Brother, art thou glad that thou shalt die in Cristin feith? Knowleche that thou hast nouȝt wel liued as thou shuldest? Art thou sori therfor? Hast thou wil to amend the, ȝif thou haddist space of lif? Leuist thou in God, Fader Almighti maker of hevene and of erthe? Leuist thou in the Fader and Sone and Holi Gost, thre persons and on God? Leuest that oure Lord Jesus Crist Godis Sone of hevene ... suffrid pine and deth, for oure trespas ...? Thankest thou him therfor? Leuist thou that thou may nouȝt be sauid but throw his deth?"

The patient having answered these questions in the affirmative, the priest proceeds:

"Wil thi soule is in thi bodi, put alle thi trust in his passion and in his deth, and thenke onli theron and on non other thing." Then he offers short prayers, conceived in the same spirit, which the dying man is taught to repeat after him.

The following prayers for the departed occur in the Burial Office of 1549:

" We commend into thy hands of mercy, most merciful Father, the soul of this our brother departed, *N.*'

" Grant, we beseech thee, that at the day of judgement his soul and all the souls of thy elect, departed out of this life, may with us and we with them fully receive thy promises, &c.'

" Grant unto this thy servant that the sins which he committed in the world be not imputed unto him, but that he, escaping the gates of hell, and pains of eternal darkness, may ever dwell in the region of light," &c.

In the Communion Service of 1549 the Intercession for the dead still finds a place in the canon :

'We commend unto thy mercy (O Lord) all other thy servants which are departed hence from us with the sign of faith, and now do rest in the sleep of peace: Grant unto them, we beseech thee, thy mercy, and everlasting peace, and that, at the day of the general resurrection, we and all they which be of the mystical body of thy son, may altogether be set on his right hand," &c.

At the celebration of the Holy Communion when there is a burial of the dead Ps. xlii, was the introit ; the collect was nearly as it now stands in the Order for Burial ; the Epistle was 1 Thess. iv. 13-18, and the Gospel, St. John vi. 37-40.

PAGE 191.

Liturgy of St. Basil (Swainson, p. 76) Εὐχὴ ἀντιφώνου γ΄. Ὁ τὰς κοινὰς ταύτας καὶ συμφώνους ἡμῖν χαρισάμενος προσευχάς, ὁ καὶ δυσὶ καὶ τρισὶ συμφωνοῦσιν ἐπὶ τῷ ὀνόματί σου τὰς αἰτήσεις παρέχειν ἐπαγγειλάμενος, αὐτὸς καὶ νῦν τῶν δούλων σου τὰ αἰτήματα πρὸς τὸ συμφέρον πλήρωσον, χορηγῶν ἡμῖν ἐν τῷ παρόντι αἰῶνι τὴν ἐπίγνωσιν τῆς σῆς ἀληθείας, καὶ ἐν τῷ μέλλοντι ζωὴν αἰώνιον χαριζόμενος. The prayer appears in the same position, and without any important variant, in the Liturgy of St. Chrysostom (Swainson, p. 113).

PAGE 194.

Canon Wordsworth writes : "A design for an Anglican Pontifical was smothered by the troubles in 1640 (Cardwell, *Synodalia,* ii. pp. 595 n., 613). In 1661-2 Cosin was charged with preparing a form for the consecration of churches, chapels, and churchyards (*ib*. 668) ... but not in time for the issue of the Prayer Book (*ib*. 675, 677). This section of the work was taken up again in 1712, 1715, by Convocation (*ib*. 819), when the Hoadly business interfered with any formal ratification."

INDEX.

Accipe Spiritum Sanctum, 204, 206, 208 f.
Act of Uniformity, first, 8 f., 14, 114.
Actio nuptialis, 151.
Adrian I, 98.
African Church, 130; "African" canons, 149 f.
Ἀγάπη, 77 f.
Agatho, 45.
Agenda, 122.
Agnus Dei, 109, 113, 118 f.
Alcuin, 54, 99.
Amalarius, 101.
Ambrose, St., 40, 149.
Ambrosian liturgy, 92.
Ἀναφορά, 88, 106, 109.
Anglo-Saxon names for Hours, 47.
Annulus pronubus, 150.
Antiphona, 42, 48 f.; *antiphonarium*, 16, 41, 48 f., 51 f., 102; antiphonal singing, 40.
Apostolical Constitutions, 32, 34, 86 f., 129, 196; Apostolic Hours, 28, 32.
Athanasius, St., 41; Pseudo-Ath., 36, 48; "Athanasian" Creed, 48, 62, 159.
Audientes, auditores, 128.
Augustine, St., 40, 157, 164; Augustine of Canterbury, 8 f., 44, 147; Psalter of, 48.

Bangor, 12; the Irish, 37.
Baptism, 123 f., 136 f.; creed of, 136 f.

Basil, St., 33, 34, 40, 191, 212.
Bede, 165, 178, 213 f.
Benedict, St., 39; Benedict Biscop, 45.
Benedictio, 203; *benedictio fontis*, 139, 141.
Benedictional, 194.
Betrothal, English forms of, 222.
Bibliotheca, 53.
Book of Common Prayer, 7 f.
Breviarium, breviary, 16, 54 f.
Burial rites of the ancient Church, 163.

Caesarius of Arles, 39, 91, 156.
Canon missae, 93, 106 f., 108 f., 118 f., 218.
Cantatorium, 102.
Canterbury, St. Martin's, 11, 44.
Canticles, 73.
Capitula, 40, 59, 64.
Cassian, John, 38.
Catecheses, 128, 134.
Catechumenate, 133.
Cathedral Uses, 13 f.
Celestine, 41.
Celtic Service-books, 10.
Charlemagne, 54, 98.
Χειροθετεῖν, χειροθεσία, 196.
Chrysostom, St., 33, 40; prayer of, 190 f., 223.
Churches, influence of the greater, 90 f.
"Churching," 148.
Circulus anni, 45.

P

Clement, St., 80 f; Council of Alexandria, 27, 149.
Clovesho, Council of, 178.
Codex Alexandrinus, 47.
Collect, 108; *collectarium*, 16, 53; *collectio*, 92.
Κολυμβήθρα, 129.
Comes, liber comitis or *comicus*, 102.
Commendatio animarum, 166.
Common of Saints, 57, 64, 106; of time, 87, 105.
Communio, 116.
Communion. English Order of, 114; of sick, 160.
Compatres, commatres, 140.
Competentes, 87, 128.
Completorium, Compline, 39.
Confirmation, 123, 137 f.
Consecratio, 203.
Consuetudinarium, 15.
Consummatio, 203.
Contestatio, 92.
Convocation, 69.
Coptic *Constitutions*, 130.
Cornelius, 199.
Cranmer, 12, 21, 68 f., 112, 189, 191.
Creed of Baptism, 136 f.
Cross, sign of, 145.
Cup, restoration of, 113.
Cursus psallendi or *psalmorum*, 11, 44.
Cuthbert, St., 139, 178, 185.
Cyprian, St., 28, 30, 83, 127.
Cyril, St., of Jerusalem, 84 f., 128, 216, 221.

Dead, care of the, 162 f.; prayers for the, 170, 223.
Decentius, 94.
Denuntiatio, 134.
Derby, accounts of All Saints', 17.
Didache, 27, 78 f., 124 f., 214, 220.
Dies in apertione aurium, 135.
Directorium sacerdotum, 66.

Dirige, dirge, 166.
Diurnale, 16.
Dryhthelm, 165.
Dunstan, Pontifical of, 194.
Dunwich, 11.

Easter Eve, 29, 128, 141, 180.
Egbert, 104; Pontifical of, 185, 193, 202 f.; *excerpta Egberti*, 46, 158 n
Egyptian monasteries, 36 f.
Εἰρηνικά, 176.
Ἐκτενή, 176.
Electi, 134.
Ember weeks, 201.
English baptismal offices, 144 f.; burial office, 169 f.; litany, 181, 186 f.; marriage office, 152, 222; Mattins and Evensong, 71 f.; orders, 207 f.
Enchiridion, 122.
Ephphatha, 136, 140, 144.
Episcopal offices, 192 f.
Epistolarium, 16, 101.
Evangeliarium, 16, 101.
Evensong, 71 f.

Families, liturgical, 91, 120 f.
"Farsings," 103.
Feriae, 61.
Flammeum, 150.
Freeman, Archdeacon, quoted, 23.

Gallican offices, 11, 91 f., 217.
Gallicinium, 32.
"Gang days," 178.
Gelasius, 95 f.
Geographical distribution of liturgies, 89 f.
Gloria in Excelsis, 36, 48, 108, 113, 119; *Gloria Patri*, 61 f.
Gospel Canticles, 62.
Graduale, grail, grayle, 16, 102 f., 108, 135.
Gray, Archbishop, 17.

INDEX.

Gregory the Great, 9, 95 f., 147, 164, 179 f.; Gregory of Tours, 92, 178.
Guthlac, 185.

Hermann, 189.
Hermas, 93.
Hippolytus, Canons of, 31, 34 f., 84, 131 f, 146, 200.
Homiliarius, 53 f.
Horae, 19, 211.
Hormisdas, 41.
"Hours," 23, 28 f., 32 f., 47.
Hymnarium, hymnal, 16, 53.

Ignatius, St., 40, 77, 149.
Immolatio, 92.
Imposition of hands, 196 f.
In exitu Israel, 167.
Innocent I, 94.
Instrumenta, 206.
Intercession of Saints, 183 f.
Introit, 108.
Invitatory, 50 f.
Invocation of the Holy Spirit, 109, 117, 220.
Ite, missa est, 75, 110, 118.

John Cassian, 38; John the Precentor, 49.
Jumièges Missal, 12; Pontifical, 194.
Justin Martyr, 81 f., 125 f., 215 f., 220.

Kalendar, 57, 65.
Kyrie eleison (Κύριε, ἐλέησον), 35, 88, 108, 176, 182 f.

Latin tongue, use of, 20, 83, 113.
Lauds, 39.
Lectionarius, 16, 52.
Legenda, legendarius, 16, 53.
Leo I, 95.
Leofric Missal, 12.
Lewis the Pious, 104.
Libelli ordinis, 100.

Liber Diurnus, 42; Liber Pontificalis, 41, 95.
Lindisfarne, 11.
Λιτανεία, *litania (let., laet.)*, 175; *trina*, &c., 184.
Litanies, missal, 176; Rogationtide, 177 f; St. Mark's Day, 179 f.; Easter Eve, 180; Lenten, 181; English, 181, 186 f.
Liturgical books, early Western, 96; liturgical families, 91, 120 f.
Liudhard, 9, 44.
Lucernarium, 32; *psalmi lucernarii*, 35.

Magnificat, 63.
Mamertus, 177.
Manuale, 122 f.
Marriage ceremonies, 149 f.
Marseilles, 38.
Marshall's primer, 189.
Mass, 74, 214.
Mattins, 26, 38, 60; English 71 f.
Maydeston, 66 n.
Memoriae Communes, 111.
Milan, 39.
Missa, 74 f., 106; *missae psalmorum*, 75; *missae votivae*, 111.
Missale, 16, 74, 104 f.; Missale Francorum, 202.
Monastic uses, 33, 36 f.
Monte Cassino, 53, 55.
"Mouth's mind," 169.
Mozarabic offices, 92, 144, 221.
Μύρον, 129.
Musaeus, 96.

Nicaea, canons of, 89.
"Nicene" Creed, 108.
Nicolas I, 151.
Nocturns, 38, 60.
Nunc dimittis, 63.

Offertorium, 108.
Oratio, 62.

Orders, validity of English, 208 f.
Ordinale, 16, 57, 65 f.
Ordinarium missae, 106 f., 115 f.
Ordines Romani, 101, 133, 193, 200.
Ordo, 101; ordo ad faciendum catechumenum, 134 f.
Osmund, 14.

Paranymphi, 150.
Passionale, passionarius, 16, 53.
Passover, 76.
Pastorale, 122.
Pater noster, 188 f.
Paul the Deacon, 54.
Paulinus of Nola, 96.
Pax, 94, 108, 154.
Perpetua, Acts of, 83.
Φωτισμός, 126.
Pica, "pie," 16, 57, 66 f.
Placebo, 166.
Polycarp, 157.
Pontifex, 192.
Pontificale, 192; Egbert's, 185, 193, 202 f.; Dunstan's, 194.
Poore, R. de, 15.
Portiforium, "portehors," 55, 57.
Postcommunio, 110.
Praefatio missae, 92.
Prayers for the dead, 170, 223.
Preces, 60; preces pacificae, 176.
Prime, 39.
Primer, prymer, 19, 212.
Processio, 177.
Processionale, 174 f.
Processions in mediaeval England, 172 f.; abolished, 174.
Proficiscere anima, 161.
"Proper of time," 57, 59, 63 f., 105; "of saints," 57, 64, 106.
Propria, 110.
Prosa, 103.
Psalms, recitation of, 37.
Psalter, 47 f., 57 f.
Purgatorius ignis, purgatory, 164 f.
Purification of women, 146 f.

"Quicunque," 48, 62, 159.
Quignon, 67 f., 70.

Redditio symboli, 131, 138.
Regiones suburbicariae, 95.
Renunciation before baptism, 128, 136.
Responsoria, responds, 43, 51.
Responsoriale, 51.
Rituale, 122.
Ritus canendi, 45.
Rogationtide, 177 f., 179.
Roman Church, clergy of (251 A.D.), 199; Greek-speaking in the first days, 93.
Roman Hours, 39; Mass, 82 f., 93 f.; Ordinations, 200 f.

Sacramentale, 122.
Sacramentarium, sacramentary, 16, 100 f.; Leonian, 97, 99; Gelasian, 97 f.; Gregorian, 97 f., 100.
Sanctorale, 66, 68.
Saints, common and proper of, 57, 64, 106.
Sarum, Use of, 13 f.; breviary, 57, 67; missal, 107 f.; manual, 123; processional, 172 f.; pontifical, 194 f.
Schola cantorum, 43, 201.
Scrutinia, 134 f.
Sees, influence of the greater, 89.
Sequentia, sequence, 103.
Sermologus, 53.
Service-books, cost of, 17 f.; purification, 23 f.; revision, 24; simplification, 20 f.; unification, 15 f.
Silvia, 32 f., 35, 130 f., 212 f.
Simplicius, 97.
Spiritus septiformis, 137.
Sponsalia, espousals, 151 f.
St. Mark's Day, 179 f.; St. Martin's, Canterbury, 11, 44.
Statuta antiqua ecclesiae, 199, 202.

INDEX.

Stratton, church accounts of, 17.
Structure of hour offices, 59 f.
Sulpicius Severus, 91.
Συνάξαι, 176.
Sursum corda, 83, 88 f., 108.

Te Deum, 48, 60, 62.
Temporale, 63 f., 66, 68.
Ter sanctus, 83.
Tertullian, 28 f., 126 f., 149, 156, 220 f.
Theodore of Canterbury, 10.
Tituli, 43.
Tractus, tract, 103.
Traditio symboli, 140.
Troperium, troper, 16, 103.

Ὕμνος ἑωθινός, 48.
Unction of the sick, 156 f., 161 f.

Uniformity, first Act of, 8 f., 14, 114.
Uses, diocesan, 13 f.

Velatio nuptialis, 151 f.
Veni, Creator, 107, 205 f., 208.
Venite, 50, 59, 63.
Vespers, 60, 62.
Victor, 93.
Vienne, 177.
Vigilius, 107.
Vigils, 29 f.
Visitation of the sick, 155 f., 222.
Voconius, 96.
Votive masses, 111.
Vulgar tongue, use of, 113.

Walafrid Strabo, 184.
Wearmouth, 45.
Winchelsey, Archbishop, 17.

THE END.

OXFORD: HORACE HART
PRINTER TO THE UNIVERSITY

PUBLICATIONS

OF THE

SOCIETY FOR PROMOTING CHRISTIAN KNOWLEDGE.

PUBLICATIONS

OF THE

SOCIETY FOR PROMOTING CHRISTIAN KNOWLEDGE.

	s.	d.
Aids to Prayer. By the Rev. DANIEL MOORE. Printed in red and black. Post 8vo. ....*Cloth boards*	1	6
Authenticity of the Gospel of St. Luke (The). Its bearing upon the Evidences of the Truth of Christianity. Five Lectures by the late Bishop of Bath and Wells. Small Post 8vo. ....*Cloth boards*	1	6
Being of God, Six Addresses on the. By C. J. ELLICOTT, D.D., Bishop of Gloucester and Bristol. Small Post 8vo. ....*Cloth boards*	1	6
Bible Places; or, The Topography of the Holy Land. By the Rev. Canon TRISTRAM. With Map and numerous Woodcuts. Crown 8vo. ....*Cloth boards*	4	0
Called to be Saints. The Minor Festivals Devotionally Studied. By the late CHRISTINA G. ROSSETTI, Author of "Seek and Find." Post 8vo. ....*Cloth boards*	5	0
Case for "Establishment" stated (The). By the Rev. T. MOORE, M.A. Post 8vo. *Paper boards.*	0	6
Christians under the Crescent in Asia. By the Rev. E. L. CUTTS, B.A., Author of "Turning-Points of Church History," &c. With numerous Illustrations. Crown 8vo. ....*Cloth boards*	5	0
Christus Comprobator; or, The Testimony of Christ to the Old Testament. Seven Addresses by C. J. ELLICOTT, D.D., Bishop of Gloucester and Bristol. Post 8vo. ...*Cloth boards*	2	0

Church History in England.
From the Earliest Times to the Period of the Reformation. By the Rev. ARTHUR MARTINEAU, M.A. 12mo. ....*Cloth boards*   3   0

Church History, Sketches of.
From the First Century to the Reformation. By the late Rev. Canon ROBERTSON. With Map. 12mo. ....*Cloth boards*   2   0

Daily Readings for a Year.
By ELIZABETH SPOONER. Crown 8vo...*Cloth boards*   3   6

Devotional (A) Life of our Lord.
By the Rev. E. L. CUTTS, B.A., Author of "Pastoral Counsels," &c. Post 8vo. ....*Cloth boards*   5   0

Face of the Deep (The).
A Devotional Commentary on the Apocalypse. By the late CHRISTINA G. ROSSETTI, Author of "Time Flies." Demy 8vo. ....*Cloth boards*   7   6

Golden Year (The).
Thoughts for every Month, Original and Selected. By EMILY C. ORR, Author of "Thoughts for Working Days." Printed in red and black. Post 8vo.   *Cloth boards*   1   6

Gospels, the Four.
Arranged in the Form of an English Harmony, from the Text of the Authorised Version. By the late Rev. J. M. FULLER, M.A. With Analytical Table of Contents and Four Maps. ....*Cloth boards*   1   0

Great Truths and Holy Lives.
A Series of Bible Lessons, from Advent to Trinity. By LADY HAMMICK. Post 8vo. ....*Cloth boards*   2   0

History of the English Church.
In short Biographical Sketches. By the late Rev. JULIUS LLOYD, M.A., Author of "Sketches of Church History in Scotland." Post 8vo. ......*Cloth boards*   1   6

Land of Israel, The.
A Journal of Travel in Palestine, undertaken with special reference to its Physical Character. By the Rev. Canon TRISTRAM. With two Maps and numerous Illustrations. Large Post 8vo. ....*Cloth boards* 10 6

Lectures on the Historical and Dogmatical Position of the Church of England.
By the Rev. W. BAKER, D.D. Post 8vo. *Cloth boards* 1 6

Martyrs and Saints of the first Twelve Centuries.
Studies from the Lives of the Black-letter Saints of the English Calendar. By Mrs. RUNDLE CHARLES. Crown 8vo. ....*Cloth boards* 5 0

Paley's Evidences.
A New Edition, with Notes, Appendix, and Preface. By the Rev. E. A. LITTON. Post 8vo. *Cloth boards* 4 0

Paley's Horæ Paulinæ.
A New Edition, with Notes, Appendix, and Preface. By the Rev. J. S. HOWSON, D.D., Dean of Chester. Post 8vo. ....*Cloth boards* 8 0

Peace with God.
A Manual for the Sick. By the Rev. E. BURBIDGE, M.A. Post 8vo. ....*Cloth boards* 1 6

"Perfecting Holiness."
By the Rev. E. L. CUTTS, B.A. Post 8vo. *Cloth boards* 2 0

Plain Words for Christ.
Being a Series of Readings for Working Men. By the late Rev. R. G. DUTTON. Post 8vo. *Cloth boards* 1 0

Readings on the First Lessons for Sundays and Chief Holy Days.

    According to the New Table. By the Rev. PETER YOUNG. Crown 8vo. ....*In two volumes*   6 0

Religion for Every Day.

    Lectures for Men. By the Right Rev. A. BARRY, D.D. Fcap. 8vo. ....*Cloth boards*   1 0

Seek and Find.

    A Double Series of Short Studies of the Benedicite. By the late CHRISTINA G. ROSSETTI. Post 8vo. *Cloth boards* 2 6

Servants of Scripture, The.

    By the late Rev. JOHN W. BURGON, B.D. Post 8vo. *Cloth boards*   1 6

Sinai and Jerusalem: or Scenes from Bible Lands.

    Coloured Photographic Views of Places mentioned in the Bible, including a Panoramic View of Jerusalem, with Descriptive Letterpress. By the Rev. F. W. HOLLAND. Demy 4to. *Cloth, bevelled bds., gilt edges*   6 0

Some Chief Truths of Religion.

    By the Rev. EDWARD L. CUTTS, B.A., Author of "St. Cedd's Cross," &c. Crown 8vo. ....*Cloth boards*   2 6

Spiritual Counsels; or Helps and Hindrances to Holy Living.

    By the late Rev. R. G. DUTTON, M.A. Post 8vo. *Cloth boards*   1 0

Things Lovely; or, The Ornaments of the Christian Character.

    By the Rev. CLEMENT O. BLAKELOCK, M.A. Post 8vo. ....*Cloth boards*   1 0

FOR PROMOTING CHRISTIAN KNOWLEDGE. 5

	s.	d.

Thoughts for Men and Women.
THE LORD'S PRAYER. By EMILY C. ORR. Post 8vo.
Limp cloth 1 0

Thoughts for Working Days.
Original and Selected. By EMILY C. ORR. Post 8vo.
Limp cloth 1 0

Three Martyrs of the Nineteenth Century.
Studies from the Lives of Livingstone, Gordon, and Patteson. By Mrs. RUNDLE CHARLES. Crown 8vo.
Cloth boards 3 6

Time Flies; a Reading Diary.
By the late CHRISTINA G. ROSSETTI. Post 8vo.
Cloth boards 2 6

True Vine (The).
By Mrs. RUNDLE CHARLES. Printed in red and black. Post 8vo. ....*Cloth boards* 1 6

Turning-Points of English Church History.
By the Rev. EDWARD L. CUTTS, B.A., Vicar of Holy Trinity, Haverstock Hill. Crown 8vo. *Cloth boards* 3 6

Turning-Points of General Church History.
By the Rev. E. L. CUTTS, B.A., Author of " Pastoral Counsels," &c. Crown 8vo. ....*Cloth boards* 4 0

Verses.
By the late CHRISTINA G. ROSSETTI. Small Post 8vo. ....*Cloth boards* 3 6

NON-CHRISTIAN RELIGIOUS SYSTEMS.

This Series furnishes in a brief and popular form an accurate account of the great Non-Christian Religious Systems of the World.

Fcap. 8vo, cloth boards, 2s. 6d. each.

BUDDHISM—BEING A SKETCH OF THE LIFE AND TEACHINGS OF GAUTAMA, THE BUDDHA.
By T. W. RHYS DAVIDS, M.A., Ph.D. With Map.

BUDDHISM IN CHINA. By the Rev. S. BEAL. With Map.

CHRISTIANITY AND BUDDHISM. A COMPARISON AND A CONTRAST.
By the Rev. T. STERLING BERRY, D.D.

CONFUCIANISM AND TAOUISM.
By Professor R. K. DOUGLAS, of the British Museum. With Map.

HINDUISM. By Sir M. MONIER WILLIAMS, M.A., D.C.L. With Map.

ISLAM AND ITS FOUNDER. By J. W. H. STOBART. With Map.

ISLAM AS A MISSIONARY RELIGION. By C. R. HAINES. (2s.)

THE CORAN—ITS COMPOSITION AND TEACHING, AND THE TESTIMONY IT BEARS TO THE HOLY SCRIPTURES.
By Sir WILLIAM MUIR, K.C.S.I., LL.D., D.C.L., Ph.D.

THE RELIGION OF THE CRESCENT, OR ISLAM; ITS STRENGTH, ITS WEAKNESS, ITS ORIGIN, ITS INFLUENCE.
By the Rev. W. ST. CLAIR TISDALL, M.A., C.M.S. (4s.)

THE HEATHEN WORLD AND ST. PAUL.

This Series is intended to throw light upon the Writings and Labours of the Apostle of the Gentiles.

Fcap. 8vo, cloth boards, 2s. each.

ST. PAUL IN GREECE. By the Rev. G. S. DAVIES. With Map.

ST. PAUL IN DAMASCUS AND ARABIA.
By Rev. G. RAWLINSON, M.A., Canon of Canterbury. With Map.

ST. PAUL AT ROME.
By the late Very Rev. C. MERIVALE, D.D., D.C.L. With Map.

ST. PAUL IN ASIA MINOR AND AT THE SYRIAN ANTIOCH.
By the late Rev. E. H. PLUMPTRE, D.D. With Map.

CONVERSION OF THE WEST.

A Series of Volumes showing how the Conversion of the Chief Races of the West was brought about, and their condition before this occurred.

Fcap. 8vo., cloth boards, 2s. each.

THE CELTS.
By the Rev. G. F. MACLEAR, D.D. With Two Maps.

THE ENGLISH.
By the above Author. With Two Maps.

THE NORTHMEN.
By the above Author. With Map.

THE SLAVS.
By the above Author. With Map.

THE CONTINENTAL TEUTONS.
By the late Very Rev. Dean MERIVALE, D.D., D.C.L. With Map.

ANCIENT HISTORY FROM THE MONUMENTS.

This Series of Books is chiefly intended to illustrate the Sacred Scriptures by the results of recent Monumental Researches in the East.

Fcap. 8vo., cloth boards, 2s. each.

ASSYRIA, FROM THE EARLIEST TIMES TO THE FALL OF NINEVEH.
By the late GEORGE SMITH, Esq., of the British Museum.

SINAI: FROM THE FOURTH EGYPTIAN DYNASTY TO THE PRESENT DAY.
By the late HENRY S. PALMER, Major R.E., F.R.A.S. With Map. A new and revised edition by the Rev. Professor SAYCE.

BABYLONIA (THE HISTORY OF).
By the late GEORGE SMITH, Esq. Edited and brought up to date by the Rev. A. H. SAYCE.

PERSIA, FROM THE EARLIEST PERIOD TO THE ARAB CONQUEST.
By the late W. S. W. VAUX, M.A. A new and revised edition by the Rev. Professor A. H. SAYCE.

THE FATHERS FOR ENGLISH READERS.

A Series of Monographs on the Chief Fathers of the Church, the Fathers selected being centres of influence at important periods of Church History and in important spheres of action.

Fcap. 8vo, cloth boards, 2s. each.

LEO THE GREAT.
By the Rev. Canon C. GORE, M.A.

GREGORY THE GREAT.
By the Rev. J. BARMBY, B.D.

SAINT AMBROSE: his Life, Times, and Teaching
By the Ven. Archdeacon THORNTON, D.D.

SAINT ATHANASIUS: his Life and Times.
By the Rev. R. WHELER BUSH. (2s. 6d.)

SAINT AUGUSTINE.
By the Rev. E. L. CUTTS, B.A.

SAINT BASIL THE GREAT.
By the Rev. RICHARD T. SMITH, B.D.

SAINT BERNARD: Abbot of Clairvaux, A.D. 1091-1153.
By the Rev. S. J. EALES, M.A., D.C.L. (2s. 6d.)

SAINT HILARY OF POITIERS, AND SAINT MARTIN OF TOURS.
By the Rev. J. GIBSON CAZENOVE, D.D.

SAINT JEROME.
By the Rev. EDWARD L. CUTTS, B.A.

SAINT JOHN OF DAMASCUS.
By the Rev. J. H. LUPTON, M.A.

SAINT PATRICK: his Life and Teaching.
By the Rev. E. J. NEWELL, M.A. (2s. 6d.)

SYNESIUS OF CYRENE, Philosopher and Bishop.
By ALICE GARDNER.

THE APOSTOLIC FATHERS.
By the Rev. Canon SCOTT HOLLAND.

THE DEFENDERS OF THE FAITH; or, The Christian Apologists of the Second and Third Centuries.
By the Rev. F. WATSON, D.D.

THE VENERABLE BEDE.
By the Right Rev. G. F. BROWNE.

LONDON:

NORTHUMBERLAND AVENUE, W.C.; 43, QUEEN VICTORIA STREET, E.C.
BRIGHTON: 129, NORTH STREET.
NEW YORK: E. & J. B. YOUNG & CO.

www.ingramcontent.com/pod-product-compliance
Lightning Source LLC
Chambersburg PA
CBHW031737230426
43669CB00007B/379